T0316579

Cambridge Elements ≡

Elements in Leadership
edited by
Ronald E. Riggio
Claremont McKenna College
Georgia Sorenson
Churchill College, University of Cambridge
in partnership with
Møller Centre, Churchill College
International Leadership Association

LEADING THE FUTURE OF TECHNOLOGY

The Vital Role of Accessible Technologies

Rebecca LaForgia
The University of Adelaide

CAMBRIDGE
UNIVERSITY PRESS

University Printing House, Cambridge CB2 8BS, United Kingdom

One Liberty Plaza, 20th Floor, New York, NY 10006, USA

477 Williamstown Road, Port Melbourne, VIC 3207, Australia

314–321, 3rd Floor, Plot 3, Splendor Forum, Jasola District Centre,
New Delhi – 110025, India

79 Anson Road, #06–04/06, Singapore 079906

Cambridge University Press is part of the University of Cambridge.

It furthers the University's mission by disseminating knowledge in the pursuit of
education, learning, and research at the highest international levels of excellence.

www.cambridge.org
Information on this title: www.cambridge.org/9781108707152
DOI: 10.1017/9781108751223

First published 2020

A catalogue record for this publication is available from the British Library.

ISBN 978-1-108-70715-2 Paperback
ISSN 2631-7796 (online)
ISSN 2631-7788 (print)

Cambridge University Press has no responsibility for the persistence or accuracy of
URLs for external or third-party internet websites referred to in this publication
and does not guarantee that any content on such websites is, or will remain,
accurate or appropriate.

Leading the Future of Technology

The Vital Role of Accessible Technologies

Elements in Leadership

DOI: 10.1017/9781108751223
First published online: November 2020

Rebecca LaForgia
The University of Adelaide

Author for correspondence: Rebecca LaForgia,
rebecca.laforgia@adelaide.edu.au

Abstract: There is presently a view that accessible technologies offer an inclusive and humanistic expression of technology. They do. But that is not all. Accessible technologies offer more than this: they contain within them lessons on transformational leadership. Through examining six case studies the reader will begin to interpret these accessible technologies as expressions of leadership. The risk inherent in the current view is that to view accessible technologies only as examples of humanism, or the good, is to risk underselling them. In fact, accessible technologies (which are being created across international society) represent a powerful leadership approach to technology itself. Through their leadership, these accessible technologies demand and create new and original thinking by society. The reader will benefit from this Element by learning to identify transformational leadership within accessible technological creations and consequently gaining a capacity to apply this leadership to the very purposes of technology itself.

Keywords: Leadership, Technology, Accessible, Stories, Future

ISBNs: 9781108707152 (PB), 9781108751223 (OC)
ISSNs: 2631-7796 (online), 2631-7788 (print)

Contents

Introduction

Figure 1. Wassende maan
Warren de la Rue and Beck & Beck Smith (Source: Rijksmuseum, Amsterdam)

This Element provides to leaders and the public the conceptual and imaginative power to engage with, to judge, and to employ in order to lead technology in an inclusive and peaceful manner.

Leadership is present in all major human endeavours: in wartime and in peacetime, during economic success and downturn, in political turmoil and stability, and within industries, schools, healthcare, and local, national, and international society. Wherever individuals are, questions of leadership arise. In the twenty-first century, a significant and as yet underexplored leadership question concerns how leadership will be present within technology. How will human leadership function within this major societal change?

It is clear that there will not be one definitive approach or answer to the question of leadership and technology (Wilson, 2004). Technology has many aspects and elements to it, and it is a complex and evolving social phenomenon. As noted by Wilson (2004), there will be leadership questions within the technology community, for example in Silicon Valley, and there will be wider leadership questions in terms of technology, for example, regarding automation or retention of the workforce. Indeed, there will be questions of technology in almost all social endeavours, including in the educational context or in future weapons production, or in the way commerce will develop. Society will face questions of leadership and technology in a range of different areas and contexts.

Given the enormity of the impact of technology on society, the purpose of this Element publication is to offer one cutting-edge idea: a contribution to the conceptualisation of leadership and technology. To introduce the core question that this Element considers, I want to start with a story that illustrates the specific problems that leadership faces regarding its interaction with technology.

This story on leadership is told by the chief executive officer (CEO) of Microsoft, Satya Nadella, and it was recorded in a book by technology expert Tim O'Reilly (2017, p. 353). The story goes like this. Satya Nadella speaks about the future of technology and, in doing so, draws on a comparison with the inspirational leadership provided by President Kennedy when President Kennedy announced the aim of landing on the moon. Satya speaks about the moon landing as being 'grand, inspiring' (O'Reilly, 2017, p. 353; see also Nadella, Shaw & Nichols, 2017, chapter 8). The symbolism of the moon is clear. Satya is creating a visual metaphor to describe how the future of technology requires an inspiring and common vision.

O'Reilly then invites Satya to provide an example of what such an inspirational common aim would be (O'Reilly, 2017, p. 353). O'Reilly reports as follows:

> [Satya] spoke movingly of his disabled son. 'I have a special needs kid, and he's locked in, and so I always think, "Wow, if only he could speak". And I think about what a brain–machine connection could do. Someone who's got visual impairment could see or someone who's got dyslexia could read. This is finally that technology that truly brings inclusiveness' (O'Reilly, 2017, p. 353).

Here we have a stunning two-part story about the future of technology. The metaphor of a moon landing works to provide the imagery of a need to aim towards something. Then, the personal story and reflections that Satya shares provide the image of inclusiveness and accessible technology. In short, inclusiveness provides the purpose, a destiny, or a metaphoric moon to aim for. To restate Satya's point, technology's purpose could be to aim for inclusiveness through accessible technology. This aim, or destination, is unreservedly endorsed and accepted in this Element as an excellent aim for the future of technology.

So, what is missing then from this story? What needs to be added to assist in the leadership of technology for this inspiring purpose?

In the telling of the story, what is missing is that while the examples are poignant, miraculous examples of the change that can occur when technology is created for inclusiveness and accessibility, there is a sense of accessibility being about an individual's life. Of course, this is true. Being able to read or write creates a great change in a dyslexic person's life. Others, such as non-dyslexic people may feel great empathy and happiness at this state of affairs. But what about non-dyslexic people – do they *themselves* share a direct relationship with the accessible technology? To restate this question: beyond the referred sense of happiness on behalf of the dyslexic person, what direct relationship does the non-dyslexic person have with accessible technology?

Because of the power of the moon metaphor, we can all visualise this destiny. (On the background to this visual metaphor see also Nadella, Shaw and Nichols [2017, chapter 8] referencing a memo from the Microsoft Research Lab at Cambridge written by Christopher Bishop who argued for "interrelated moon shots".) The power of this visual metaphor is that we can all see the moon, and we can all imagine the journey and destination of landing on the moon. I want to show in this Element how, in a similar manner, leading the creation of technology that assists the dyslexic in reading or writing, or leading a range of other creations for the blind, visually impaired, or hearing impaired, is in fact like landing on the moon, *a common destination*.

I will argue that there is a direct relationship with accessible technologies *regardless of who you are*. We all have a direct stake in accessible technology and inclusiveness. Without being able to see this common purpose or a common relationship to accessible technology, it becomes almost impossible for the leaders of technology to galvanise support for inclusiveness and accessibility as a universal and common aim for technology itself.

To examine this common relationship that we all have with accessible technology, the correct tools are required. The first section of this Element provides these. Section one then closes by demonstrating that accessible technologies (artefacts) contain within themselves an aspect of transformational leadership, that of inspirational motivation (Bass & Riggio, 2006, p. 6). In Section two, general inspirational motivational symbols and stories contained within each of the accessible technologies are drawn from around the world and include instances from Israel, Spain, Switzerland, Netherlands, and the United Kingdom. The prism of transformational leadership is crucial to unlocking the story contained within each of the accessible technologies examined. It is through the prism of leadership that it is possible to see these accessible technologies as a generalised statement, as an inspirational movement to a common 'future state' (Bass & Riggio, 2006, p. 6). This Element is about evoking the visual, the metaphors, the symbols contained within these technological creations so that the inspirational leadership that forms part of each of these accessible artefacts can be seen. It is important to note, the purpose of outlining these accessible technologies is not to explain their design, function or product description. I have not the expertise to judge the artefacts from that perspective. The descriptions are to capture their symbolic significance—that is, the leadership stories, as I interpret them, contained in these artefacts.

Section three reflects on how these accessible artefacts and the leadership lessons they contain contribute to the understanding of authenticity in the context of transformational leadership. Last, Section four takes the leadership lessons from this Element and applies them in the context of a Google hypothetical technological leadership dilemma. In summary, it shows how the leader who creates accessible technological creations (or artefacts) is creating an inspirational future for all. This publication offers no original theory or synthesis of leadership. Rather, it engages with an existing leadership approach – that of transformational leadership. The cutting-edge element is apparent in how this leadership publication uses this traditional approach. It uses the particular aspect of inspirational motivation to chip away at and uncover the hidden inspirational leadership for all that is embedded in accessible technologies. The result is in accordance with the observations below:

> In a criticism of the state of leadership studies, Alvesson and Deetz (2000: 52) wonder if Yukl's (1989) agenda to define 'What is Leadership' could have misled leadership research. They suggest that more might be learned from questions regarding 'what can we see, think, or talk about if we think of leadership as this or that?' (Parry & Hansen, 2007, p. 282).

This Element provides real-life and yet imaginative and creative examples of technology and leadership to 'see, think and talk about' (Parry & Hansen, 2007, p. 282). In Section two, the lessons from accessible artefacts are rich and evoke an inspiring future in which, for example, we comprehend the diversity in each other; become more aware of our thinking; observe public spaces change and expand through the alchemy of light and sound; hear our name called again and again, creating a sense of community; listen to others in humility; witness unconditional public participation; and are invited to participate in the future. All these inspiring futures await the reader. At its core, this publication is a celebration for all of the symbolic and metaphoric stories of inspirational leadership that are contained within these accessible artefacts.

1. The Tools for Examining the Story of Leadership Contained in Accessible Artefacts

The role of stories in the context of leadership has been examined by Parry and Hansen (2007, pp. 283–4): 'Stories do things, they create things, bringing notions and ideas to a level where they can be represented coherently and acted upon'. Indeed, they argue that stories, because they have 'powerful and concrete effects' can 'operate and function just as leaders do' (Parry & Hansen, 2007, p. 284).

This Element is about telling the story of how accessible technologies hold within them inspiring leadership stories for the future of technology. Section two

Figure 2. Knielende figuur met hamer en beitel

Jan Toorop (Source: Rijksmuseum, Amsterdam)

records six accessible technologies, each of which is examined for its leadership story, and Section three applies these leadership lessons. However, first it is necessary to have the tools to unpack these leadership stories contained within the six accessible technologies. Therefore, Section one is dedicated to outlining the tools needed to unpack the stories of leadership contained in the accessible technologies.

Broadly, there are three conceptual tools required to unpack the leadership stories contained within the case studies that follow: first, leadership and storytelling; second, leadership and artefacts; and third, transformational leadership as a tool to examine accessible technological artefacts. Leadership and storytelling entail a broad appreciation of the connection between leadership and stories. To examine leadership and artefacts entails an overview of the literature supporting the claim that leadership values can be contained within technological creations. That is, it is possible to study and reveal leadership stories not only via human case studies but also by looking at our material creations. The literature refers to these as 'artefacts'. There is then a general and brief introduction to the multi-disciplinary area of accessible technology followed by an overview of the well-established framework of transformational leadership as outlined by Bass and Bass (2008, p. 10).

What is new and innovative about this leadership approach is *how* all the steps outlined above are then employed. These tools are used to reveal a common inspirational future contained in material technological creations. It is the use of leadership theory as a way of seeing leadership itself. Through applying an element from a pre-existing leadership approach to artefacts that are material, it is possible to see symbolically and metaphorically how these material objects lead, 'inspire', and offer a 'shared vision' (Bass & Riggio, 2006, p. 6) for all.

1.1 The Value of Story in the Context of Leadership

1.1.1 Leadership Stories are 'Sense-making' and 'Symbolic'

Stories in the context of leadership offer several advantages. They are known for 'sense-making' (Parry & Hansen, 2007, p. 287). They can also operate as 'symbols that represent organisational understanding' (Parry & Hansen, 2007, p. 287). One of the great advantages to the concepts of sense-making and symbols in the context of the leadership of technology is that we are currently in uncertain times. Therefore, considering the unknown consequences of technology and its effect on society, the desire for sense-making is paramount.

1.1.2 Leadership Stories in the Post-industrial Age:

Leadership stories of technology therefore potentially provide not only a concrete, positive dimension to future action but also a point of contrast when technology is veering towards problematic destinations. It is significant that the stories about technology and its destination are themselves made accessible and appreciable for the community at large. Without making the stories regarding technology accessible themselves, an elitism exists regarding how the development of technology will occur. Therefore, stories provide an egalitarian role in the sense-making aspect of the future of technology. The importance of stories in the context of technology has been specifically acknowledged by Watts et al. (2018, p. 290), who noted that:

> With the shift from the industrial age to the information age, organisations have been described as increasingly complex, interactive systems, requiring leadership strategies that are capable of managing the chaos (Thiel, Bagdasarov, Harkrider, Johnson, & Mumford, 2012; Uhl-Bien, Marion, & McKelvey, 2007). As organisations and their environments become more complex, the 'gray' and ill-defined situations calling for ethical decision making emerge more frequently (Mumford et al., 2008). Stories appear to provide a narrative structure that helps followers with organising, or making sense of, complex information from the organisation's past and present, such as why particular decisions were made (Boal & Schultz, 2007). Our findings indicate that stories of leadership may serve as a vehicle for the protagonists' cognitive-motivational patterns, or mental models – at least with regard to the personalized or socialized goal structures of these mental models. Because stories may be used to shape followers' perceptions and behavior by signalling what is normative and non-normative, storytelling may be a critical aspect of leadership.

This finding is intuitively correct. Since we are all individual participants in a world that will be shaped by technological creations yet to come, we will be faced with decisions regarding what is ethical or unethical, what is 'normative and non-normative' Watts et al. (2018, p. 290). Having access to stories that provide examples of ethical leadership of technology will be, as Watts et al. (2018) note, critical to providing the capacity to navigate this complexity. The proposition by Watts et al. (2018, p. 290) is endorsed with their statement that, 'story telling may be a critical aspect of leadership'.

The advantage of starting with the extract from the CEO of Microsoft, Satya Nadella, is that he has already created a story about the leadership of technology. It is a story with two parts. The first part concerns how technology requires an inspirational galvanising destination, such as President Kennedy's leadership of the moon landing. The second aspect of Nadella's story is that such an inspirational purpose resides within accessible and inclusive technologies. The storytelling has been largely done. However, the missing element of the story concerns how accessible technology might be achieved as a 'collective goal' (Watts et al., 2018, p. 277). How does everyone have a relationship with the story of accessible technology such that we can use it to navigate the future with this normative goal? Section two deals with that specific issue – which is how to draw out of a technological creation, or, as it is referred to in the literature, an 'artefact' – a common leadership story so that we can see symbolically and metaphorically the accessible technologies acting as a leader. Using the metaphoric story as told by Satya Nadella, the thesis of this Element is that accessible technologies lead as President Kennedy did. This section gives the tools to imaginatively experience the inspiring voice of general and powerful leadership emanating from these creations.

1.2 Leadership Values Are Contained within Artefacts

1.2.1 Artefacts as Containing Politics

This section concerns the tool required to extract the story of leadership from accessible technologies. Langdon Winner (1980) wrote a famous piece titled, 'Do Artifacts Have Politics?'

It is worth recapping his central thesis:

> In controversies about technology and society, there is no idea more provocative than the notion that technical things have political qualities. At issue is the claim that the machines, structures, and systems of modern material culture can be accurately judged not only for their contributions of efficiency and productivity, not merely for their positive and negative environmental side effects, but also for the ways in which they can embody specific forms of power and authority (Winner, 1980, p. 121).

It is also worth recapping Winner's example. First, he uses the atom bomb, suggesting that it is an 'inherently political artifact' (Winner, 1980, p. 131). He goes on to note that:

> Taking the most obvious example, the atom bomb is an inherently political artifact. As long as it exists at all, its lethal properties demand that it be controlled by a centralized, rigidly hierarchical chain of command closed to all influences that might make its workings unpredictable . . . The state of affairs stands as a practical necessity independent of any larger political system in which the bomb is embedded (Winner, 1980, p. 131).

Winner (1980, p. 135) considers, therefore, that we 'ought to attend more closely to technical objects themselves'.

1.2.2 Technological Artefacts and Values

The same point in terms of artefacts is made in the work of Flanagan et al. (2008, p. 322), who developed a comprehensive approach to the idea of looking to values (in the context of an experimental computer game prototype). The authors noted that:

> The idea that values may be embodied in technical systems and devices (artefacts) has taken root in a variety of disciplinary approaches to the study of technology, society and humanity (Winner, 1986; Latour, 1992; Hughes, 2004; Mackenzie and Wajcman, 1985).

The work of Flanagan et al. (2008) is significant because it gives a sense of how broad the potential is for examining values within artefacts. Listing a number of potential values, such as liberty, justice, enlightenment, comfort, trust, and sustenance (Flanagan et al., 2008, p. 322), the authors then take these values and apply them to a particular design of a prototype: 'RAPUNSEL, a large multi-disciplinary collaboration aimed at designing and implementing an experimental game prototype to promote interest and competence in computer programming among girls of middle school age, including girls from disadvantaged home environments' (Flanagan et al., 2008, p. 331). The significant point about their work is the endorsement of the pluralistic values for which artefacts can be examined. This Element examines artefacts for leadership stories rather than design values. However, the work of Flanagan et al. (2008) supports the concept that artefacts contain multiple and plural values and are therefore a rich area of study.The concept of artefacts is also employed as a method in engineering and artificial intelligence (AI) ethics, for example, in Sekiguchiand and Hori (2018). The frame of using artefacts as a method of exploration and discussion has also been used the context of International Law (Hohmann & Joyce, 2018) and Philosophy (Korsgaard, 2008, pp. 322–324). In the context of AI for engineers and design, the authors commented on the idea that 'society would be a better place if ethically designed artifacts are more clearly realised and the same artifacts change their surrounds to be more ethically valuable' (Sekiguchiand & Hori, 2018). The aim of their work was to bridge the gap 'between ethical discourse and engineering practice' (Sekiguchiand & Hori, 2018). In a similar way, the aim of this work is to bridge a gap between artefacts and the leadership ideas they contain and communicate.

1.2.3 Accessible Technology as Artefacts

The concept that artefacts can contain human values is extensively discussed by Chamberlain and Bowen (2006), specifically in the context of accessible design and accessible technology. The authors also examine images of artefacts in their work (Chamberlain & Bowen, 2006, pp. 70–71). This visual bent to the study of artefacts is significant for this Element.

The artefacts discussed in Section two are not large public sculptures or visible public displays. For example, one of the case studies is the OrCam which sits on the side of your glasses and is described as 'tiny'.[1] To evoke the values of leadership contained in these often tiny artefacts, the visual and the impressionistic are necessary to release the leadership stories that the artefacts contain. Therefore, the work of Chamberlain and Bowen (2006) is important for endorsing a creativity and freedom in the study of artefacts. The authors reinforce the point made by the writers discussed above (Flanagan et al., 2008; Winner, 1980) that 'artefacts can be effective vehicles for communication: to make statements, encapsulate ideas and illustrate knowledge' (Chamberlain & Bowen, 2006, p. 68). However, it is their overview of the role of artefacts in stimulating thinking about ideas and accessibility that is relevant to this Element. They write in the context of engineering and design, but their work is significant for how artefacts can be studied and used. For example, they state that 'Gaver and Martin (2000) apply such artefacts as a way of "mapping the design space", exploring the territory where future solutions could be positioned' (Chamberlain & Bowen, 2006, p. 68). They go on to note that:

> Design provides ways of thinking and skills that can deliver artefacts as tools for creating new scenarios of the world we live in. These scenarios can simulate unfamiliar experiences and allow users to make imaginative extensions into unfamiliar areas. Thus designers can create new 'contexts' for others to experience and explore as part of human-centred design (Chamberlain & Bowen, 2006, p. 68).

This Element is centred on leadership, not design (see generally on accessible and inclusive design, Clarkson et al., 2006). Nevertheless, Chamberlain and Bowen's (2006) approach is important for Section two of this work. The accessible artefacts are examined with the 'tool' of leadership in order to 'creat[e] new scenarios of the world we live in' (Chamberlain & Bowen, 2006, p. 68). These leadership stories from the artefacts will then 'simulate unfamiliar experiences and allow [the viewer] . . . to make imaginative extensions' (Chamberlain & Bowen, 2006, p. 68). In summary, the approach by Chamberlain and Bowen (2006) is to use the examination of artefacts with an emphasis on the visual, on the imaginative, on the future of things. This is the style of the artefact descriptions given in Section two. These artefacts are not

---

1 https://www.orcam.com/en/myeye2/

examined for their design or product description. Rather, these accessible artefacts are used to evoke a visual description that is 'stimulating' and at times imaginative, and to 'encapsulate ideas' and 'knowledge' about leadership (Chamberlain & Bowen, 2006, p. 68). The work of Chamberlain and Bowen is therefore introduced here because it supports the concept of artefacts containing values and concepts. However, their study also represents a certain style: that of using the visual description of artefacts to evoke 'stimulation' and 'imaginative extension' (Chamberlain & Bowen, 2006, p. 68). In short, their work endorses creativity in the study of artefacts.

1.2.4 Leadership and Artefacts

In the context of leadership studies, the concept of artefact has been used by Anisman-Razin and Kark (2012, p. 253), who explained that artefacts are:

> 'the phenomena that you would see, hear, and feel' (Schein, 2004, p. 23), they are intentionally made products perceived by individuals (Gagliardi, 1992) ... recent work considers them as influential factors that have a vast significance for individuals and organisations (Cappetta & Gioia, 2006; Rafaeli & Pratt, 2006).

The authors go on to note 'through the use of artifacts, individuals communicate to others who they are' (Pratt & Rafaeli, 2001). This suggests that artefacts are powerful symbols used by individuals and organisations to convey deep meaning about themselves and their desired image (Cappetta & Gioia, 2006; Anisman-Razin & Kark, 2012, p. 254). This reinforces the applicability of artefacts specifically in the area of leadership. However, this work was centred on the leadership of an individual, in this context Steve Jobs, CEO of Apple. The authors considered the individual and Jobs's attire, logo, and name (Anisman-Razin & Kark, 2012, p. 254). This Element focuses not on the study of individuals but rather on the leadership that emanates from artefacts themselves. Nevertheless, the work of Anisman-Razin and Kark (2012, p. 253) reinforces the applicability of artefacts in the area of leadership generally.

1.2.5 Conclusion on Artefacts

Given the tradition of looking to an artefact to reflect politics (Winner, 1980), values (Flanagan et al., 2008), ethics (Sekiguchiand & Hori, 2018), design, visual, and imaginative possibilities (Chamberlain & Bowen, 2006), International Law (Hohmann & Joyce, 2018) and Philosophy (Korsgaard,

2008, pp. 322–324) and leadership (Anisman-Razin & Kark, 2012), the aim in Section two is to use the approach of studying artefacts to comprehend the story of leadership that is embedded in the accessible technologies. There are six artefacts of accessible technologies dealt with in Section two. Each one of these artefacts is examined for the particular leadership story that is contained within it. The accessible technologies are not examined for their design features. They are not examined for the effect that they have on users, specifically. They are examined for the general leadership values that they contain.

So, to return to Winner (1980, p. 135), we are 'attend[ing] more closely to technical objects themselves' in order to see the 'form and quality' (Winner, 1980, p. 131) of the leadership contained within them.

A Concluding Story – Sigrid Cerf's Artefact Story: I want to end this subsection on artefacts with a story. The idea of this Element is to render the leadership of technology a 'sense-making' story of leadership for the future of technology, to ensure this is a publication accessible to anyone interested in the future leadership of technology. Although the concept of examining 'artefacts' for leadership without also examining humans is not an intuitive position, it is nevertheless a vital approach to this work which is based on the symbolic and metaphoric. As an academic mother, I generally run my work past my daughters. But in this instance, the concept of artefacts was off-putting to them. It seemed this particular word got the daughters offside. Artefacts is a reified and somewhat alienating word. This was a problem because the word and concept of artefact appeared to halt the flow of a sense-making story, and my daughters were no longer engaged, perhaps even alienated by what seemed to be a deliberately academic and obscure term.

Yet the concept was central to this whole leadership Element argument. Indeed, the title states, 'Being led by inspirational technological creations'. I was at an impasse; 'artefacts' was a central concept, but it is not a word used in everyday speech. Then, in my research I came across the story below. I thought, yes! That is 'artefact' in everyday language. Sure enough, when I told my daughters the story, they were back with me and, in fact, very keen to hear Section two. So, I share Sigrid's story below to make the concept of artefact real, and to facilitate sense-making, thus enabling me to use the term in good faith as an approach to the leadership of technology's future.

In researching for this Element, I came across the inspirational story of Vint Cerf. Cerf is Chief Internet Evangelist for Google and called the 'Father of the Internet' for his seminal part in establishing the architecture for the internet and email (Solsman, 2017) He is an advocate for accessibility and has commented that it was '[a]lmost criminal' (Solsman, 2017) that there has not been more accessible technology created. In an interview with Cerf, Solsman (2017) discussed with him the use of the technology he was a part of creating: 'Email, for one, brought Cerf more than the typical benefit of posting and interacting on your own timeline. "Because I'm hearing-impaired, emails are a tremendously valuable tool because of the precision that you get"'.

This is a compelling story of the effects of technological accessibility and brilliant creativity. However, in researching Vint Cerf, I came across his wife, Sigrid Cerf. It was *her* story that I used for my daughters as an example of the concept of artefact naturally and powerfully told.

Sigrid Cerf in an interview described the joy of listening to audio books, telephone calls, and conversations with her son and husband after fifty years of a hearing impairment. Her new-found capacity arrived via a technology called a cochlear implant, which assists people with hearing impairments (Boswell, 2010).

However, it is the following comment that struck me. Sigrid noted that, 'I was fitted with my original body-worn processor, I received an auxiliary, microphone, a cable that could be plugged into my processor. The visible presence of this cable tells people that *what they have to say to me is important to me*' (Boswell, 2010; emphasis added).

Sigrid Cerf saw this cable as something that is – while highly physical, material, and practical – also symbolic, and is therefore able to 'tell people' something. In this story, the material cable, which we can think of as a technological artefact, represents Sigrid's values, including those of listening, openness, and inclusion. This technological artefact, despite sitting in a stable and material form, is also about an imaginative future. The cable is symbolic and evokes the vision of all the important conversations yet to come, all the 'important' things yet to be said. In short, if we are able to see technological artefacts as Sigrid has, then what we see are highly visible and symbolic creations that 'tell people' something. *This is the method used in exploring the accessible artefacts in* Section two: *to simply ask what do they 'tell people' about leadership?*

After explaining the idea of artefacts with Sigrid's words and example, the concept seemed to resonate with my family. They moved from viewing artefacts as an alienating concept to a useful one. I also noted a more emotional and open expectation – they seemed keen to know what these leadership artefacts will 'tell'. But before moving to this 'telling' in Section two, there is further work to be done. There is a need to obtain a general understanding of the international movement in accessible technology and then a particular understanding of which aspect of leadership will be used as a tool to reveal the story of leadership contained in the artefacts. Both these aims are undertaken in Section 1.3.

1.3 The One Leadership Tool to Tell the Stories of Leadership in Accessible Technological Artefacts

In obtaining a general sense of the area of accessible technology, it becomes clear why examining these artefacts for the presence of transformational leadership is a logical approach. A brief overview of accessible technology as a general field follows. In this brief survey, the natural fit between transformational leadership and accessible technology will be evident. Then, the elements of transformational leadership are laid out. This does not contribute anything new, rather, it uses as the accepted foundation the work of Bass and Riggio (2006). However, what is important is that one element of transformational leadership is selected as the key tool to unpack the leadership stories contained in the accessible artefacts. In summary, at the end of Section 1.3, the reader will possess the core 'tool' (Chamberlain & Bowen, 2006) to examine the artefacts that follow.

1.3.1 Accessible Technologies Generally

There is a range of ways in which accessible technologies can be examined through the perspective of, for example, design (Clarkson et al., 2006), which makes it clear that accessibility is an open, complex, multi-disciplinary, and ongoing area of design and research:

> This book consists of papers . . . encourages considered discussion and allows the appraisal of research from a broad range of perspectives, which this year include: multi-institution funded programs into provision for older people; assistive and rehabilitation technology; computer science approaches to inclusive design and rehabilitation; housing design; engineering design of robotic assistance; product design, and social anthropology. All these are united in the common endeavour of improving the design of accessible technology (Clarkson et al. 2006, pp. v–vi).

There is also the interaction of accessibility and universal design (Steinfeld & Maisel, 2012), or the humanistic design of accessible technologies (Reha et al., 2017), or the international law on the provision of accessible technologies (United Nations Convention on the Rights of Persons with Disabilities (UN CRPD), 2006), or the World Health Organization's (2019) push towards global cooperation on assistive technologies, or the cultural awareness promoted by the Global Accessibility Awareness Day.[2]

All these approaches to accessible technologies are essential and practical; they exert genuine cultural, legal, and design leadership in their impact. They

---

2 https://globalaccessibilityawarenessday.org/

have grown from expertise, dedication, international advocacy, and persever-ance. They contain practical and real changes for those who benefit from accessibility and technology.

It is worth noting that accessibility has become a powerful normative concept and is a touchstone of international treaties such as the UN CRPD (2006). In particular, Article 9(1)(b) of this treaty provides that accessibility measures shall apply to persons with disabilities in relation to measures relating to 'information, communi-cations and other services, including electronic services' (UN CRPD, 2006). Accessibility, in terms of this human rights treaty, is a vital right; it is proactive and has a great deal to achieve in the technological age (Ellis, 2016; Greco, 2016).

The above is not a complete overview of the legal, cultural, and design push for accessibility but it does give a snapshot of the idea that this is a growing and significant area.

1.3.2 Accessible Technologies through the Prism of Leadership Rather Than through the Prism of the User, Design or Technicalities

This Element considers accessible technologies from a different perspective, looking to the general leadership stories that are contained within them. This distorts the normal analysis of accessible technologies, which are generally viewed as a site for assistance for a particular need, and they very importantly serve that purpose. The above literature (1.3.1) provides only a brief overview; it centres on this core element that accessible technologies are vital for users, and that they need to be further developed and funded. However, in this Element accessible technologies are considered from a different perspective; they are considered not for their use, but for their symbolic and metaphoric leadership stories. That is not to undermine their use, that being practical assistance to those who need them. (Please see, for example, the visual conclusion of this Element for a testimony of their profound effects on an individual who needs accessible technologies.) Nevertheless, this Element's aim is to expand the influence of accessible technologies and demonstrate that they also contain leadership lessons for all.

1.3.3 The One Leadership Tool to Chip Away at the Artefacts

There is a natural fit, at least in the first instance, between accessible technolo-gies and transformational leadership. Transformational leadership at its sim-plest is described as follows:

> But authentic transformational leaders, as moral agents, expand the domain
> of effective freedom, the horizon of conscience and the scope for altruistic
> intention. Their actions aim toward noble ends, legitimate means, and fair

consequences. Engaged as they are in the moral uplifting of their followers, in the sharing of mutually rewarding visions of success, and in enabling and empowering them to convert the visions into realities … (Bass & Steidlmeier, 1999, p. 211).

The foundational work on the frame of transformational leadership has been established by Bass and Bass (2008, pp. 618–48) and Bass and Riggio (2006). These foundational works on transformational leadership establish that there are components to transformational leadership, which include: *idealised influence*, that is, 'transformational leaders behave in ways that allow them to serve as role models for their followers' (Bass & Riggio, 2006, p. 6); *inspirational motivation*, in which 'transformational leaders behave in ways that motivate and inspire those around them by providing meaning' (Bass & Riggio, 2006, p. 6); *intellectual stimulation,* in which 'transformational leaders stimulate their followers' efforts to be innovative and creative by questioning assumptions, reframing problems, and approaching old situations in new ways. Creativity is encouraged…' (Bass & Riggio, 2006, p. 7); and *individualised consideration*, in which 'transformational leaders pay special attention to each individual follower's needs for achievement and growth by acting as a coach or mentor. Followers and colleagues have developed to successively higher levels of potential' (Bass & Riggio, 2006, p. 7).

These are the four key attributes or elements of transformational leadership. However, there is an important triage that now needs to occur before the examination of the accessible technology artefacts can begin. That is, there will only be *one* element from transformational leadership that is used in the examination of the artefacts that follows, and that is inspirational motivation. The reason that only this element is employed is now explained.

Essentially, there is one aspect to transformational leadership that is the focal point of this Element. This one significant element, which is inspirational motivation, forms the core tool to chip away at and uncover the leadership residing within the accessible technologies studied in Section two. Below is an explanation of why the other elements of transformational leadership are not relevant for the study of the artefacts.

Idealised influence, or charisma, is not relevant to the study of transformational leadership in this particular context. This is because the study of leadership concerns artefacts and not the human person. It was envisaged by Bass and Bass (2008, p. 620) that charisma would not always be a necessary element to transformational leadership: 'the charismatic leader is likely to be transformational, but it is possible – although unlikely – to be transformational without being charismatic. A highly intellectually stimulating teacher, for instance, may transform students without their regarding the teacher as charismatic'.

The next element, that of *intellectual stimulation*, is not relevant to the analysis of the artefacts that follows. Each of the technical artefacts is inherently a highly complex creation that draws upon, for example, emerging AI. Accessible technologies have an innate intellectual stimulation. They naturally create 'new approaches' (Bass & Riggio, 2006, p. 7). They are created by challenges being put to their human creators to push beyond the known boundaries of technology. As indicated at the beginning of this discussion, accessible technologies literally create miraculous thresholds and extraordinary capacities; for example, the OrCam is an artefact that can read when the visually impaired or blind person simply points at a text. The element of intellectual stimulation is therefore self-evidently present in all accessible technologies. This aspect of intellectual stimulation inherent in accessible technologies is more relevant for discussion within the design literature. It speaks to the development and technical deployment of accessible technologies, which is not the study of this Element.

The element of *individual consideration* again is self-evidently and inherently contained within each of the artefacts without further need for examination. There is a natural 'attention to each follower's needs' (Bass & Riggio, 2006, p. 7). Implicit in the accessible technologies is the fact that the needs of the user have been listened to effectively (Bass & Riggio, 2006, p. 7). In this sense, individualised consideration looks similar, for example, to the humanised design of accessible technology (Reha et al., 2017). That is, design reflects a high level of individual humanistic consideration of the needs of the user of the technology. Accessible technologies' very form speaks to an extraordinary level of individual consideration and each accessible technology necessarily links to the needs of the users: one example is a creation that responds to the need of the dyslexic student to be able to read the text. Individual consideration is in the DNA of each of the accessible artefacts. They are designed for the user. This is why accessible technologies were created: to assist and provide access for users and their particular needs. This aspect of individual consideration is the core feature of the artefact and requires no illumination. It is the very moral and ethical reason the design and the artefact came into being.

It is, however, *inspirational motivation* that is the element of transformational leadership used to examine accessible technologies. Inspirational motivation, according to Bass and Riggio (2006, p. 6), occurs when 'leaders get followers involved in envisaging attractive future states; they create clearly communicated expectations'. This is the crucial aspect for this Element on leadership – that each of the accessible technologies contains general inspirational motivation.

It is worth expanding upon inspirational motivation. Bass and Bass (2008) consider the conceptual differences between charismatic leadership and inspirational leadership. Drawing on Gardner, they note that inspirational leaders 'conceive and articulate goals that lift people out of their petty preoccupations, carry them above the conflicts that tear a society apart, and unite them in the pursuit of objectives worthy of their best efforts' (Gardner, 1965b, p. 98, cited in Bass & Bass, 2008, p. 607).

This is the underexplored aspect of accessible technologies. Inspirational motivation is the idea that the leader can project a 'future state' (Bass & Riggio, 2006, p. 6), which is inspiring, which is real, and which represents a change that their followers can 'envisage' (Bass & Riggio, 2006, p. 6). The objective in Section three is therefore to examine the accessible technological artefacts for the general inspirational motivation that they are leading towards, to examine and 'imagine' the 'future state' that they are 'envisaging'. This is the key tool, transformational leadership's quality of inspirational motivation, that will be employed to tell the story of how artefacts are leading towards an inspirational motivation for all international society. Or, to refer back to the Introduction, how each of the artefacts contains an inspirational common destiny – a moon landing for all.

It is by applying this tool of inspirational motivation from the transformational leadership approach that we can see within these artefacts the inspiring future state that they contain. In short, it is this element of transformational leadership that shifts the capacity of the accessible artefact from the category of liberating one particular individual who can use the technology (an incredibly significant aim) to a category that also includes being an inspiring vision for all.

1.4 Summary of Section One

In summary, this section has provided the tools to examine the technological artefacts presented in Section two. Gladwell has spoken of the importance generally of "tools" in developing and engaging thoughts. The attempt of this section was to provide such tools. (Gladwell, n.d., sec. 22 lesson three) The first tool described was the re-enforcement of the value of story in the context of leadership. It was established that telling the general story of leadership and technology is significant. This is because a story helps the 'sense-making' (Parry & Hansen, 2007, p. 287) of complexity and an unknown future, and provides ways of galvanising to a common end.

The next tool introduced the idea of the artefact as containing politics (Winner, 1980), values (Flanagan et al., 2008), ethics (Sekiguchiand & Hori, 2018), visual and imaginative possibilities (Chamberlain & Bowen, 2006), and leadership

Figure 3. Omslagontwerp voor: Wendingen, 1931
Mommie Schwarz (Source: Rijksmuseum, Amsterdam)

(Anisman-Razin & Kark, 2012). The proposition that a material object can express a value, a political association, or a leadership position was established. The story of Sigrid Cerf rendered the intellectual discussion real; thus, the section on artefacts and the examination of accessible technologies could be summarised simply using the question, what do they 'tell people' (Boswell, 2010) about leadership?

This was followed by a general introduction to accessible technologies, outlining the fact that there is an international movement to create accessible technologies from a variety of disciplinary perspectives, including international law, international cultural awareness, international health perspectives, and the design community. The common element among all the different disciplinary perspectives is that accessible technologies are inherently about transformational and liberating change.

Therefore, there is a very natural fit between the aim of accessible technologies and transformational leadership. Given that innate relationship, there is a logic to examining accessible artefacts for the transformational leadership that they contain. Section one has considered how transformational leadership comprises four elements (Bass & Riggio, 2006, pp. 6–7). However, it is the element of inspirational motivation that is the key tool. And the key question to ask of each of the accessible artefacts is, where do they contain inspirational motivation? Asking and answering this question is the aim of Section two.

2. The Leadership Stories Contained in the Six Accessible Artefacts

2.1 Introduction

This section contains six examples of accessible technological artefacts. Each artefact is examined for the presence of inspirational motivation, one of the elements of transformational leadership. The six artefacts are from different geographical regions, including Israel, Spain, the United Kingdom, Switzerland, and Netherlands. Yet, even though they are geographically diverse, each artefact exhibits a common, two-fold theme of accessibility and a leadership story of inspirational motivation in which the artefacts point towards 'unite[d]' (Gardner, 1965b, p. 98, cited in Bass & Bass, 2008, p. 607) 'attractive future states' (Bass & Riggio, 2006, p. 6), which is an inspirational destination for international society.

Each artefact is briefly described, with the aim of giving a visual impression. This Element is not a design study of accessible technologies nor is it a product assessment. This is a leadership story. The objective is to have a visual sense of the artefact and then to step back and, instead of asking the normal questions regarding such artefacts, for example, regarding their design or their use, we can envisage something else, which is a broader story of leadership towards an inspirational future for all.

As discussed in Section one and in the introduction to this section, each of these accessible artefacts contains a transformational leadership vision that transcends individual use or design and speaks to an inspirational future. The importance of seeing the implicit leadership contained within these artefacts is that it enables us to start to gather examples of transformational leadership as contained within accessible technologies. Gathering these examples enables a charting towards a future in which technology can be guided to achieve a common inspirational aim of creating accessible technologies for all. This idea is introduced in Section four.

Section three, which follows the examination of these six artefacts, gives a sense of how having the capacity to understand the leadership contained within these accessible technologies can help to guide future leaders. But first, before looking to future scenarios, this section gathers together the six examples of accessible artefacts that contain inspirational motivation and transformational leadership.

2.2 Sonocent Artefact

The first artefact of accessible technology is the Sonocent Audio Notetaker. The technicalities of this technology will naturally evolve and the description which follows is not a description of the technologies capabilities. It is rather a glance, an impression or a snap shot- an image as I see it. Indeed by the time you are reading this, new features may well be created for the technology, and indeed all the other artefacts that are subjects of study in this work. This study is seeking to be timeless. It is a study of artefacts as symbols of leadership. Seeking to capture the metaphoric and the symbolic the technologies. The intriguing aspect of this technology is that it 'turns audio into visual blocks', which 'can then be structured using coloured highlighting and combined with images and text notes'.[3]

These chunks or blocks of recordings can also be coloured and highlighted according to how important one specific part of the audio is to the listener. So, for example a screen could be a coloured-building-block representation of all the audio moments of a lecture.

Subsequently, these audio blocks can be edited and turned into words via transcription technology. A whole range of activities can be conducted with the audio, including adding images and PowerPoint slides.[4] However, this study is not of design, and not of the technicalities of using this technology. This is a study of artefacts and their symbolic contribution to leadership. So, the question could be asked, what does this artefact tell me about leadership, or, more precisely, 'what is the general inspirational motivation here for all of us who may look at these coloured blocks of audio?'

Although we are not concerned with individuals and this is a study of the symbols contained in artefacts, it is worth noting what was said by the CEO of Sonocent, Mr Dave Tucker: 'Imagine you're about to embark on a degree in music on your first day ... You ... notice your classmates ... start frantically marking blobs on their pages ... You ... slowly fill with anxiety ... for any one of the over 100,000 ... University students in the UK with dyslexia, this scenario may feel familiar' (Tucker, 2015). Tucker was clearly empathising with the difficulty experienced by people with dyslexia, who, despite being highly creative (Cancer et al., 2016), can experience challenges in 'taking comprehensive notes in class' (Garbutt, 2019).

---

3 https://en.wikipedia.org/wiki/Sonocent
4 https://sonocent.com/audio-notetaker/#audio-notetaker-demo

What is the inspirational motivation when we look to the artefacts of these coloured blocks of audio? What we see is the representation of sound, information, words, and knowledge *not* in a written form. We see, through the coloured blocks, literacy before it is born as a word-style symbol. We see literacy and knowledge as a physical block. The information, the knowledge, the words simply look like the rectangular building blocks with which a child might play. The image is inviting and cubist; the blocks are small, long, and of different colours, and they can be arranged.

The inspirational motivation here is that this technological artefact has achieved, for all people who view it, a different representation, a diverse representation of literacy. The artefact shows literacy before it is contained in a word symbol. In this sense, it is an accessible technological artefact that is a symbol of diversity. It provides an artefact of a different way of engaging with knowledge and literacy. It stands functional and proud, symbolically composed of different colours and shapes. The coloured blocks, could potentially educate all who look at them, about the nature of thinking and the diverse relationships that people have with literacy. Looking at the Sonocent coloured blocks, there is no requirement for empathy for the person with dyslexia or diverse thinker. Empathy is not the lesson here. The coloured blocks are more breathtaking. They are a visual representation of different ways of thinking about literacy – of having a coloured sound block to represent literacy before there is even a hint of the written symbol of a word.

I interpret the visual representations of Sonocent as inspiring. Like looking at a work of art by Cézanne, who was said to have introduced into the world of painting a new form that moved from the literal and realist approach to capture a wholly different way of representing the world. He introduced the idea of doubt into art:

> The Renaissance admired an artist's certainty about what he [or she] saw. But with Cézanne as the critic Barbara Rose remarked [that] ... 'This is what I see' becomes replaced by a question: 'Is this what I see?' You share his hesitations about the position of a tree or branch ... Doubt becomes part of the painting's subject. Indeed the idea that doubt can be heroic, if it is locked into a structure as grand as those of the paintings of Cézanne ... (Hughes, 2012, p. 18).

So, too, the vision of the building blocks, in which information is represented as coloured blocks of thought, reveals to the observer the natural diversity in the human mind. In a creative manner it introduces doubt into the subject of knowledge and literacy. Sonocent, through its visual artefact of accessible technology, provides an inspirational representation of diversity. It convinces, through its physical manifestation, the different architecture that exists in peoples' minds. It represents and envisages an inspirational future in which technology will represent diversity. It is a shared experience, even for those who do not possess this diversity of thought and cannot engage with the building blocks and the audio representation of knowledge. The general viewer is potentially able to see and be educated about pluralism—of thought and of how people experience the information around them.

Once we think of this accessible technological artefact as containing this shared inspirational moment, it becomes clear how much we lose if we think of Sonocent as only an accessible technology for a select group of people, such as those with dyslexia. We lose the extraordinary inspirational teaching moment that simply looking at this technology offers to anyone; they can see, like in a work by Cézanne, a representation of literacy and thinking as different, as open, as diverse, as 'heroic' (Hughes, 2012, p. 18).

To obtain insight into the architecture of different modes of thinking and processing is to be provided with a rich visual experience. In learning to see accessible technologies as artefacts that speak to all, we are led towards a society that naturally asks the following questions. How does it feel to have that different architecture in the processing of information? Perhaps it leads society to ask of others, how are you processing and listening to what I am saying? Perhaps it asks us to think about how we process and think in terms of literacy and information.

In short, what it does is to encourage an increased consciousness about our own thinking processes and about how we engage with those around us. That is, one of the core aspects of this accessible technology is that it creates a distance or doubt over what we implicitly accept as a 'normal' experience in terms of processing information (Ellis, 2016). This is a particular type of thinking, politics, or engagement. It encourages an expansion of our questions, of our knowledge, and of our engagement with the other. The transformational leadership that Sonocent provides is an *inspirational motivation* to envisage a future in which diversity of thinking is understood and our own thinking is reflected upon – in short, to create more consciousness about how we think.

2.3 OrCam Artefact

The OrCam was created in Israel (Cohen, 2016). It is a highly sophisticated and advanced form of accessible technology. The OrCam can be visualised as a small USB – a little black piece of plastic. However, it is far from inconsequential, despite being quite tiny (Dillet, 2017). It is a device that can be clipped onto the side of eyeglasses; once clipped on, it performs a number of extraordinary actions. These actions are described on the OrCam website. Some of the attributes of this technology are briefly described below.

'Voice-activated device that provides increased independence by communicating visual information, audibly. With OrCam MyEye, you can read text, recognize faces, identify products & more'. https://www.orcam.com/en/

To recall, the purpose of these artefact case studies is not to describe the function or design of particular technologies, which by their nature continually evolve. Rather, the case studies are employed to consider the leadership story, which can be interpreted from reflecting generally or metaphorically on the artefact.[5]

What then is the inspirational motivation contained in this small black artefact? I am going to centre on the facial recognition feature. What is the inspirational motivation contained in this facial recognition? It is, of course, for the individual user who is sight impaired or blind, a radical new capability to call the name, perhaps, of an approaching person, to greet them in a coffee shop, or to call them over. We can imagine a woman sitting in a coffee shop hearing the name of her sister, whispered into her ear by the OrCam, as her sister arrives, or a husband hearing the name of his wife as she approaches. The OrCam enables both to welcome—the sister and wife—to call them over to sit and be together, or simply to remain silent and experience the added moments of anticipation as their loved one arrives.

But what is the inspirational motivation for all? For those of us not needing to hear the names of our sister or wife in the imagined coffee shop? One of the first things to note is that this is a radically different image of the use of technology and facial recognition compared with for example a dystopian style facial recognition in the context of armed drone viewing in which there is a sense of technology being above and the viewed person being below. (Chamayou, 2015, pp. 37–45) and (Kalpouzos, 2018, p. 120). In contrast the use of facial recognition in the OrCam context, as imagined above, is for engagement and community- that is for a name to be called. The inspirational motivation from this artefact is a sense of deep unity (Gardner, 1965b, p. 98, cited in Bass & Bass, 2008, p. 607), a 'future state' (Bass & Riggio, 2006, p. 6) in which there is an inspirational aim that is not based on conflict. The OrCam, as an inspiring leader of technology, 'carries' us above 'conflict' (Gardner, 1965b, p. 98, cited in Bass & Bass, 2008, p. 607) and moves us into community.

When we look to this accessible technology, we can see that the sense of inevitability and a dystopian future normally involved in facial recognition has been broken (see also examples in Nadella, Shaw & Nichols, 2017, p. 200).

---

5 https://www.orcam.com/en/about/

Here, facial recognition is used for community, to call a name, to greet a friend, to have a future in which we are all 'involved' (Bass & Riggio, 2006, p. 6). The accessible technological artefact is offering an inspirational 'expectation' (Bass & Riggio, 2006, p. 6) of technology as a symbol of engagement and humanism, of unity, and of peace. Unlocking the general inspirational leadership and symbolism of this artefact enables it to claim its' power and role as a counter point to other symbols. So for example the armed drone ' . . . is . . . a symbol, a myth, a fixture in our imagination' (Kalpouzos, 2018, p. 120). Through seeing the general inspirational leadership in Orcam, and indeed other similar artefacts, it can be a powerful part of our collective imagination. The use of technology is common between both artefacts in that both look for another; but in the case of the OrCam the artefact looks in order to call their name. Again, we can imagine what might be lost if we think only of the OrCam as applicable to those who need to clip it onto their glasses. The OrCam stands as a symbolic transform- ational leadership example for all, an example of how we can use technology to metaphorically call each other's names, to be in peaceful community. This is the broad inspirational motivational future evoked by this accessible artefact.

2.4 Visualfy Artefact

The next accessible technological artefact is Visualfy and it is made in Spain. It is described on its website in the following terms: 'Doorbell, alarm clock, baby, alarms . . . a world of important sounds is turned into colours, so you can relax and enjoy being home. For people with hearing loss and technology fans'.[6]

This artefact symbolically performs an extraordinary alchemy. It takes sounds and then translates them into light or colour. The website states that, 'We have developed a unique algorithm, based on artificial intelligence, that recognises sounds and translates them into visual alerts on any connected device. We work every day to improve the algorithm and develop applications that can add even more value'.[7]

In addition to its personal use, Visualfy can also be adapted to respond to the sounds in workspaces and public places.[8] This is an evolving product with 'soon-to-be-launched' translation of further sounds. However, recall that design and function are not the focus or ambit of this study. We are concerned with the symbolic, the metaphors, the stories of transformational leadership themes.

Visualfy performs the alchemy of translating sound into vision. It does this in private and public spaces. In the context of public spaces, this is not done by generating more physical construction or people than in the private context. It is

---

6 https://www.visualfy.com/   7 https://www.visualfy.com/about-us/
8 https://www.visualfy.com/visualfy-places

the technology itself that creates the extraordinary transformation of a public space through the act of taking pre-existing sounds and translating them into light. This is an inspirational use of technology in public spaces.

Visualfy is working metaphorically as an architect on our public spaces, potentially redesigning them. Visualfy is an architect of space – it is expanding space and translating urbanised sounds. It inspires a future in which the public architecture, the architecture of everyone – and this includes those who use and those who admire Visualfy – expands towards inclusion.

Therefore, the three artefacts examined – Sonocent, OrCam, and Visualfy – have exhibited transformational leadership by providing inspirational motivation around values such as diversity of thought and increased consciousness of our thinking, the use of technology to call each other's names to create community, and the redesign and expansion of public spaces for inclusion. If these technologies had only concerned design or use, then the common future that they speak of would have been more difficult to describe. Instead through examining these artefacts for their impressions and symbols of leadership, it is possible to see their more timeless contributions to inspirational values. This section has focused on permitting these accessible artefacts to speak of a general future, allowing them to generate the inspirational leadership that is within them. Regardless of whether you might need Sonocent, OrCam, or Visualfy, inspirational leadership is about a future in which you can see diversity and a heightened awareness of your own consciousness and thoughts about knowledge (Sonocent), about a future in which you are being greeted and gain an increased sense of community (OrCam), and about public architecture and remoulding (Visualfy). As stated at the beginning of this Element, we are accustomed to thinking about the world-changing consequences of armed drones or the atom bomb, despite probably never having had an interaction with these weapons. The purpose of this Element is to celebrate accessible technologies and to liberate them from being understood as a particular subset of technology, instead allowing them to be understood as a general inspirational future for all. We can then start to think about the future leaders of technology, asking, 'How does this creation encourage accessibility and an inspirational future for all?'

The next three artefacts discussed appear to be three disparate events – examples of what we might essentially call 'good technological inventions'. However, they have at their core a commitment to accessibility in a broad sense. They are examples of asking and answering the question, how does this creation encourage accessibility and an inspirational future for all?

The three artefacts are the book as reconceived by the Accessible Books Consortium (ABC) in Geneva; the Rijksmuseum in Amsterdam, which offers inspirational leadership through openness and accessibility; and the Vodaphone Mobile Classroom, which creates accessible education for refugee camps. Each of these is still an artefact, and a material creation. These examples offer further illustration of the transformational leadership through technology, by creating inspirational and motivational futures.

2.5 Accessible Books Consortium: Accessibility through Reconceiving the Artefact of a Book

The Accessible Books Consortium (ABC) is housed within the World Intellectual Property Organization (WIPO). The ABC works with government agencies, commercial publishers and not-for-profit organisations. The purpose of the ABC is to 'provide training, technical assistance and funding for educational materials in national languages to be used by primary, secondary, and university students who are print disabled' (ABC, n.d.c).

Before discussing the elements of inspirational motivation and leadership evident in the ABC, it is important to set some context. As the ABC has noted, the global need for accessible books is overwhelming:

> Some 253 million people worldwide are visually impaired, according to the World Health Organization's 2017 estimates. More than 90% of these are resident in developing countries, where the World Blind Union (WBU) estimates that people who are blind have only a 1 in 10 chance of going to school or getting a job. The lack of accessible books is a very real barrier to getting an education and leading an independent, productive life. The WBU estimates that less than 10% of all published materials can be read by blind or low-vision people (ABC, n.d.a).

The ABC works with a number of stakeholders, such as governments, to engage in important projects and produce accessible books. For example, in Sri Lanka, the ABC has, along with funding provided by the government of Australia, been 'able to convert over 1,000 educational books into accessible formats in one year, an incredible accomplishment considering that similar NGOs produced approximately 100–200 books over the same period' (ABC, n.d.c).

This remarkable difference, the ABC notes, was caused by the availability of electronic files of the books produced (ABC, n.d.c). This enabled the DAISY (Digital Accessible Information System) Lanka Foundation (DLF) to produce accessible books efficiently in Sri Lanka. The ABC states that in the past 'NGOs have had to scan every page of hard copy books' (ABC, n.d.c), and that 'organisations have used human narrators to record audio books' (ABC, n.d.c). The important point to note is that 'both of these processes are resource intensive. Using the original electronic files provided by commercial publishers, however, DLF was able to convert books into accessible formats more efficiently and economically' (ABC, n.d.c).

The ABC is not simply an ad hoc humanitarian organisation. It is part of the implementation of a significant international treaty, the Marrakesh Treaty to Facilitate Access to Published Works for Persons Who Are Blind, Visually Impaired or Otherwise Print Disabled (WIPO, 2016). The Marrakesh Treaty came into force in September 2016 (ABC, n.d.a, 2018) and enables 'the production and transfer of accessible books across national boundaries' (ABC, n.d.a). Therefore, the ABC can be seen as a practical, functioning body supporting the implementation of an international treaty.

More broadly, what we see here is a story of leadership creating accessibility. International diplomatic leadership existed in the creation of the Marrakesh Treaty (WIPO, 2016). Further leadership existed in the creation of the ABC within the WIPO, and yet more in amassing the connections among stakeholders, for example, in the case study of capacity development regarding the ABC's work with Sri Lanka, the DLF, and the Australian government. Moreover, this leadership was present in the innovative use of technology in which electronic files enabled the accessible delivery of books that would otherwise have been inaccessible. At every point along this road, leaders – wherever they were placed – were asking how technology could promote accessibility.

2.5.1 ABC Books Are 'Born Accessible'

One of the core transformational leadership lessons lies in the ABC's work in terms of changing the expectations and culture in the publishing industry more generally. A specific aim of the ABC is to influence and generate accessible publishing (ABC, n.d.b). Essentially, the ABC has a distinct aim of promoting 'the production of "born accessible" publications that are fully accessible to all readers – our vision is for the same product to be usable by everybody' (ABC, n. d.b). The ABC wishes to generate a culture for publishers in the initial production of a book in such a way that the books are immediately accessible to all – transformational leadership influencing the very conception of a book (ABC, n. d.a), so that it is 'born accessible' (ABC, n.d.b).

The significance apparent in the discussion above concerns how the ABC has used its leadership and cultural influence to generate the idea that books should be 'born accessible'. In relation to this concept, at the London Book Fair the ABC received an international excellence award that 'recognizes outstanding leadership and achievements in advancing the accessibility of digital publications for persons who are print disabled' (ABC, n.d.b).

It is important to recall that the term 'visually impaired' includes not only those who are blind and visually impaired but also those who suffer from dyslexia or other disabilities related to text (WIPO, 2016). Through its provision of inspirational motivation for all in this context, ABC exhibits transformational leadership in a profound manner. The consortium has gone back to the birth of the book to project a future state in which books will be born accessible – a state that expands the very concept of accessibility. The term 'born accessible' implicitly presumes there is no 'perfect form' to which accessibility is added. Rather, ABC leadership is re-orientating society's idea of the perfect form for the book. The perfect book is one that is born accessible.

2.5.2 Inspirational Motivation

One of the core leadership lessons from the ABC is a new understanding of the perfect possible form in which books could be born, such that non-accessible books appear lacking and incomplete in comparison. Thus, the artefact of the traditional book is not the perfect form. The ABC, in its very core mandate, is negating the idea that a book as traditionally understood is sufficient. The general inspirational motivation contained in this artefact is that of a gentle cultural change in language and expectations. Therefore, when we look to the everyday non-accessible book, it will appear, through the influence of the ABC, incomplete, not all it could be. This is inspirational leadership via the enabling of our everyday artefacts (the books) to be examined anew. We can see how they could be more. This is a future therefore of possibilities; what we think of as the perfect form may infact be contingent. It is difficult to argue that the humility that comes from such knowledge is inspirational. Humility and inspiration do not necessarily sit together. However, I want to insist that humility can be inspirational. For example, Handler et al. observed 'I would also insist on the power of social science methodology to push us beyond our personal politics or situations, to enforce a form of humility in which we must listen to voices other than our own' (Handler et al., 2005, pp. 483–4). The ABC operates as transformational leadership for all, via implicitly rendering current ideas of what might constitute publishing or a book as imperfect or lacking((Koskenniemi, 2001, pp. 506–507). We can now see, in the traditional book, elements of non-accessibility. The ABC therefore does create an inspirational motivational future, in which we see contingency and therefore have a heightened sense of what could be.

2.6 The Rijksmuseum as an Artefact: A Metaphor for Inspirational Outreach

The next example of an artefact concerns the Rijksmuseum in Amsterdam, which is considered an exemplar of open access for artwork (Dijkshoorn et al., 2014, p. 7; Pekel, 2014).

To understand the seminal nature of the Rijksmuseum's decision to open and release its collection in a digital form to the public domain, it is important to first understand the background to the decision. Sanderhoff (2017) describes the context of the Rijksmuseum's images being increasingly available online, in poor quality and in the absence of licencing. Sanderhoff (2017) further observes that, 'Others would have seen a violation of rights. The Rijksmuseum saw an opportunity ... They invited people to re-use images for all imaginable purposes, from illustrating scholarly publications and Wikipedia articles to remixing them for new design objects ... '.

This describes a form of accessible leadership in which the management of the Rijksmuseum has made artworks – which previously one needed to travel to Europe, and specifically to Amsterdam, to view – accessible in high quality to all (who have access to the internet). The image of accessibility via technology is clear. At one stage, artwork was available to those who could afford to go to the Rijksmuseum; now it is publicly available to all. Further, the Rijksmuseum has created the Rijksstudio, which enables people from all over the world to participate in creating their own version of online collections of the Museum's master works, thereby adding even a further extra element of accessibility and participation (Dijkshoorn et al., 2014, p. 7).

In an exchange organised by Adelaide University, in 2017, I was seconded to the World Trade Organisation (WTO) in Geneva for a short placement. However, it is important to understand two facts that relate to this secondment. The first is that the secretariat of the WTO is, importantly, a neutral body. This is important because the WTO services its member states; that is, it is not partisan or political and it offers a neutral and professional service (Cottier, 2007, p. 497; 2010). However, my research interest concerned my background in writing about the importance of opening up international trade and creating increased transparency and public participation (LaForgia, 2015, pp. 145–54) – in short, making international trade information, dialogue, discourse, decisions, and outcomes accessible to the public.

Therefore, when I was making my final presentation to the WTO, I was faced with a dilemma: it was important that I was able to speak respectfully about openness while at the same time not demand levels of political engagement that were not appropriate for the secretariat. Consequently, I used the Rijksmuseum as a leadership example, an artefact of institutional openness and transparency. In the opening section of my presentation, I drew an analogy between access to an art institution that had previously been limited by its geography and access to the WTO for the general public. Access to the museum has now radically transformed into a context that is meaningful, in the sense that it is open, freely available, and given engagingly by the institution (Pekel, 2014).

This inspirational change of accessibility provided a profound shift in the institutional character of the Rijksmuseum – a shift from a geographically contained museum to one that actively reached out to the limitless followers that would be interested and moved by its artwork. In short, the Rijksmuseum's very institutional character was profoundly changed by its decision to become accessible. This 'self-perception' (Qizilbash, 2009, pp. 251–2) transformed the museum to one that 'saw potential to build relationships with all the people out there' (Sanderhoff, 2017).

This was the core point I was seeking to make in my presentation at the WTO – that the character of the institution changes when it decides to become radically accessible and reach out actively and meaningfully to its limitless followers (Hirsch, 2008, p. 291; Qizilbash, pp. 251–2; Koskenniemi, 2001, p. 506). Therefore, concepts such as transparency, openness, and accessibility are important not just for those who now view the artwork but also because the institution itself changes; it becomes an institution that is interested and potentially connected with limitless others. A type of "constant expansion" (Koskenniemi, 2001, p. 506).

In this way, the Rijksmuseum operates as an inspiring leadership artefact. It is a relevant and profound artefact that demonstrates what accessibility through technology can achieve. When transformational leadership through technology is performed successfully, it works as providing inspirational motivation or as a living metaphor that can be translated effectively to other institutional contexts. The artefacts of leadership therefore work not simply within its own genre or context of accessibility but also as a transferable metaphor. This accessible artefact (the Rijksmuseum) has the potential to affect parallel and disparate institutions and contexts. It works as a transferable metaphor, or as an example that can speak easily to different contexts (as I found was the case in the context of my oral presentation discussing and explaining the importance of accessibility and institutional character as presented at the WTO).

2.7 The Vodafone Mobile Classroom as Accessible Leadership: Authentic Artefacts Invite More Participation

The last case study concerns my attendance in a non-official capacity at a meeting, the Gender Dimension of E-commerce, held on 27 April 2017 at the UN in Geneva, Switzerland. Among the speakers was Joakim Reiter, Group External Affairs Director of Vodafone (UN Conference on Trade and Development, 2017). During the meeting, Reiter spoke about Vodafone's outreach activities in education. After the meeting, I pursued this topic. The project concerned Vodafone's 'instant schools' (Vodafone Group, 2016) or, as the project is known, the mobile classroom. As stated by Vodafone, 'It is estimated that the Vodafone Foundation's work in refugee settlements will benefit at least 62,000 children and young people by the end of 2016 and the Foundation is targeting up to three million children and young people in refugee settlements by 2020' (Vodafone Group, 2016).

The mobile classroom is essentially a wheeled suitcase. The classroom is contained in a box with wheels and a handle that can be pulled up. The wheels enable the box to be pulled along. The box weighs 52 kilograms and is made of hard, grey, protective material. Within the box are twenty-five tablets that have been loaded with 'educational software, a projector, a speaker and a hotspot modem with 3 G connectivity' (Collins, 2015). Further, this classroom has its own power supply, which enables it to be 'charged as a single unit from one power source in six to eight hours, after which it can be used for an entire day without access to electricity' (Collins, 2015). The classroom can be assembled within 20 minutes (Collins, 2015).

The Vodafone mobile classroom can be viewed as an artefact (Anisman-Razin & Kark, 2012). The box encompasses old technologies, for example, the idea of the hard or robust outer case that protects the precious educational materials from sun or sand, and the tablets loaded with, 'old' materials, which enable the skills of literacy, mathematics, and philosophy. This combination of old with new forms of technology, including tablets and power generation, demonstrates a physical artefact of transformational leadership, through containing inspirational motivation.

This physical artefact symbolises the profound change that can be made to children's lives. It provides them with accessible educational opportunities they would not otherwise have encountered. This is done via the merging of technology designed in a practical and accessible manner. This form of inspirational motivational leadership is different from the inspiring leadership metaphor described earlier in the discussion of the Rijksmuseum artefact. This is inspirational leadership in a box, which can be physically 'unveiled' (Collins, 2015), and which can be touched, opened, and engaged with. So often, technology is ephemeral. It seems to exist 'out there', in a sense, to be beyond control. Yet, through creating such a powerful artefact, technology becomes something hardy and robust. This is significant not only because it locates or explains technology for us, but also because it creates an artefact that provides both a challenge and an invitation. The box works as inspirational motivation – an aspect of transformational leadership creating an ethical challenge or question for the international community.

The challenge operates in two stages. Through the construction of a physical artefact – that is, the box – we are symbolically invited to reflect on what we could possibly put into the box to make it even more accessible. The inspirational leadership apparent in this artefact works as a conceptual challenge, as an invitation to be involved. Through the very physical form of the box, we are symbolically invited to think and reflect upon what technology we might add. For example, there are laptops in this box currently, but perhaps they are not loaded with, for example, dyslexic-friendly audio translations of books, or with software that can translate speech into text. Thus, the form of the box is inspirational, in that it envisages a future in which we are all invited to participate creatively and to contribute.

In unclipping the artefact of the box, and imaginatively 'looking into it', our minds are naturally attuned to the broad question of what might be added. Therefore, this last artefact illuminates the fact that the artefacts of leadership can work to symbolise a future in which we are invited to participate, a future in which we have opportunities for service. The leadership artefact also works symbolically to remind us that there is always work to do, and more to be added to the artefact.

2.8 Conclusion: The Elements of Accessible Leadership

This section has taken six case studies that illustrate the contours of the inspirational leadership contained in accessible technological artefacts. The core idea is that by travelling through the creations from Israel, Spain, Netherlands, the United Kingdom, and Switzerland, it is possible to see the inspirational leadership that is occurring in accessible artefacts, and that each one of these creations has a set category of users and those it wishes to serve. However, each artefact is also a general inspirational story of leadership. Each artefact holds inspirational aims for all: to increase knowledge about diversity and consciousness (Sonocent), to enable more greetings and community participation (OrCam), to redesign our public spaces through alchemy (Visualfy), to generate a humility so we can listen more to others (ABC), to create a meaningful metaphor for creative and open public engagement

(Rijksmuseum), and to challenge us to participate in the future of technology (Vodafone box). Section three revisits the leadership scholarship, exploring the contribution of the inspirational leadership contained in these accessible artefacts to themes within leadership. Then, in Section four, the power of this idea of accessibility being a driving aim for technological leadership is explored through a hypothetical case study inspired by Google.

3. Reflection on Leadership Lessons Learned from Case Studies

So far, we have six technological artefacts that have been examined using the tool of inspirational motivation, derived from transformational leadership. This tool or lens of inspirational motivation has enabled these artefacts to take on a level of generality, a sense of a wider story. Therefore, we saw examples of artefacts that speak to and educate about diversity, we saw artefacts that provide peaceful alternatives for facial recognition in our societies and communities, and we saw artefacts that reform and expand public spaces through the alchemy of light and sound. These technological artefacts speak of values and ideals that are inherently inspirational. We also saw in the artefacts broad social values being applied through the use of accessible technology. As examples, the outreach of the Rijksmuseum, enables artworks to be viewed throughout the world; education and power is contained within a sturdy box and wheeled into refugee camps; and lastly, the very form and content of the book is being moulded so that it can reach out and include many more people.

3.1 The Twin Approach of Leadership in Creating Accessible Technological Artefacts

The essence of the technology leadership derived from the six case studies can be found in the facilitation of two questions to be posed by the leader. The leader will ask how technology can be used to generate more accessibility. For example, the leader may ask, How can technology be a part of delivering accessible education, artwork, health products, and security? The values that are to be made accessible are essentially unlimited and will be determined by where the leader is leading. For example, an art museum will ask the question of art, while a health innovator will ask it of access to health products. The leader will then be able to see the inspirational 'future state' they are aiming for. Is it to expand respect for diversity, for more public space, for inclusion? In short, leaders of technology are aware that the accessibility question will guide them to deliver both the particular technology – for example, to the dyslexic or the blind person – and the general inspirational leadership to all. The leaders of technology are aware with each creation they produce and then lead in technology that they have not only a general inspirational duty but also a particular duty for accessibility. They have their chart plotted to the inspirational moon, as posited by Satya Nadella at the beginning of this work.

In asking this conceptually simple but directed question of 'accessibility', the leader will achieve a balance. The question, if answered well, will achieve practical technological designs and functions. So, for example, the art museum will deliver art works accessibly to the world, via the internet. However, the accessibility question also sustains the aspirational desire to create ethical technological developments. Leadership through creating accessibility aspires to the twin aims of practical and inspirational outcomes. Thus, through achieving practical and aspirational aims, leadership in creating accessible artefacts is an important conceptual tool for the leader in the twenty-first century.

This style of leadership perceives technology not simply as an opportunity but also as a responsibility. The leader is looking to enhance and expand opportunities for technology to create accessibility. For the leader, therefore, accessibility becomes a new lens through which to view technology and, at the same time, it becomes a benchmark from which to assess leadership. This form of leadership also makes some interesting contributions to existing frames of reference in the leadership field. These are outlined below.

3.2 A Lack of Circularity in the Concept of Accessible Leadership

Antonakis (2018), has been critical of 'loaded' terms used in recent leadership approaches that 'include the outcome in their definitions ...' (Antonakis, 2018, p. 68). It is worth providing the quotation in full, and addressing the concerns it raises:

> Terms like *transformational, authentic, ethical* and the like suggest an outcome – that is that the leader transforms or is morally good. Doing so, is problematic from a scientific point of view (van Knippenberg & Sitkin, 2013) for three reasons: constructs should not be defined by their outcomes, because doing so leads to tautologies and circular theorising (MacKenzie, 2003); the nature of what is measured should be exogenous with respect to the outcomes it is supposed to cause (Antonakis et al., 2016); and scientists should separate ideological agendas from accurately describing how the world works (Antonakis, 2017; Eagly, 2016) (Antonakis, 2018. p. 68).

The inspirational motivations contained in the accessible artefacts is protected, however, from this claim of 'circular theorising'. Unlike the terms 'good' or 'ethical', the question of accessibility is an innately practical construct. So, when we refer back to the examples described earlier, the artwork either is or is not accessible, the mobile classrooms either do or do not work and books are either born accessible or they are not. This is in contrast with words such as 'ethical' or 'good', which can lead to circular theorising. For example, I might claim that I am an ethical leader or that my technology is ethical, yet that may be highly debatable. I could claim an AI weapon or an Armed Drone is ethical because it is precise (Chamayou, 2015). This is a highly debatable claim and raises serious questions such as, Who defines the enemy and who ensures the precision is measured after an attack? (Chamayou, 2015) However, in stark contrast, regarding the claim that inspirational leadership exists within an accessible artefact, the actual technological creation creates a symbolic and real-world experience or a truth as to whether the leader has successfully engaged with technology to increase accessibility and whether the technology does create an inspirational future state. There is no need to contort reasoning or to argue for the ethics of accessible artefacts; they are known as ethical through their very aims and their inspirational, motivational values (Korsgaard, 2008, p.323).

3.3 The Authentic Nature of Accessible Leadership

The concept of authenticity in leadership is a seminal one. In the early years of transformational leadership, profound discussion about whether the so-called 'evil leaders' could be transformational leaders led to the following conclusion by Antonakis (2018, p. 66):

> Bass (1985) directly built on Burns's (1978) theory. Bass extended the model to include subdimensions of what he termed *transformational* (instead of transforming) leadership. Also, although in Bass's original conceptualisation of transformational leadership he was not concerned with moral and ethical overtones, he eventually came around to agreeing with Burns that the likes of Hitler were pseudo transformational and that at the core of veritable transformational leadership were 'good' values (see Bass & Steidlmeier, 1999).

The concept of good in the tradition of transformational leadership is expressed as 'authenticity': 'The element of transformational leadership that usually best distinguishes authentic from inauthentic leaders is individualised consideration. The authentic transformational leader is truly concerned with the desires and needs of followers and cares about their individual development. Followers are treated as ends, not just as means (Bass & Steidlmeier, 1999)' (Bass & Riggio, 2006, p. 14).

Each of the leadership artefacts discussed in Section two is naturally concerned with 'individualised consideration' (Bass & Riggio, 2006, p. 14). As discussed in Section one, individualised consideration is in fact a prerequisite; it is a necessary element in the very creation and identification of the accessible leadership challenge. For example, to develop the mobile classroom, it was necessary to identify first the individualised needs of the children in the refugee camp. In the context of Vodafone, in part this was achieved through linkages with the United Nations High Commissioner for Refugees. Transformational leadership, by creating inspirational motivation through accessible artefacts, naturally requires a specific identification to address this individualised consideration.

In the context of the Rijksmuseum, before an outreach idea could be conceived, it was necessary for the organisation to consider art enthusiasts and the general public who did not have access to the physical Rijksmuseum in Amsterdam. Again, individualised consideration was a necessary precondition for grappling with the accessibility and technology issues.

Thus, a change in the equation in terms of authentic transformational leadership is evident here. Instead of individualised consideration being an aspirational marker in the context of accessible artefacts, it is a necessary precondition: 'Followers are treated as ends not just as means' (Bass & Riggio, 2006, p. 14) because it is their ends that define the creative accessible project with which the leader is seeking to engage.

As Bass and Riggio (2006, p. 16) note, there is still work to be undertaken in the context of authentic leadership:

> Clearly, and as Burns (1978) emphasised, the morality of transformational leadership is critical. Throughout our discussion of transformational leadership, we assume for the most part we are speaking of authentic transformational leadership. Yet it is clear that much work needs to be done to better understand the dynamics of authentic leadership, in general, and authentic transformational leadership in particular.

This is the core contribution offered by accessible artefacts and the inspirational leadership that they contain. Each artefact is a contribution to this 'dynamic' between the general and the particular expression of authenticity (Koskenniemi, 2001, pp. 504–506). The particular expression of authenticity is in the accessible creation itself: in the actual outreach, in the empowerment contained in the delivery of opportunity. The general authenticity is contained in the inspiration that the artefact holds for society generally: in the six case studies there were the values of diversity, community, inclusive public spaces, humility and listening to others, and public engagement and participation. These are general visions that are an expression of authentic leadership. The dynamic of the general and the particular is set as a natural dynamic in the context of accessible artefacts (Koskenniemi, 2001, pp. 504–506). Therefore, it would appear that accessible technological artefacts are oriented towards creating the expression of authentic leadership.

However, one final and vital element from transformational leadership needs to be considered. As Burns (1978, p. 36, cited in Hollander, 2012, p. 285) stated, 'Only the followers themselves can ultimately define their own true needs'. This profound observation by Burns is the key element of empowerment and it will provide the ultimate test for authenticity in the context of accessible artefacts and the inspirational leadership contained therein. Empowerment is not and cannot be an imposed concept (Koskenniemi, 2001, pp. 504–506). Empowerment is relational. It is offered in good grace by the leader who has created the accessible artefact or creation. To sincerely take individuals as they are and to generate opportunities for empowerment via access to books, education, or artwork is to offer the individuals a choice. There is no force, there is no presumption, there is no compulsion in accessible artefacts, because true empowerment has an element of freedom embodied within it. There is no compulsion to accept the general inspirational future in which there is open public participation and in which one can study the old masters at the Rijksmuseum; but, should they have a desire to do so, the public can be empowered in the inspirational future of open participation in the visual and aesthetic history of major artists that is now available.

3.4 Reflections on Leadership, Not a Synthesis

Section three has reflected on lessons learned from the artefacts discussed in Section two. It is clear that leaders of technology can use accessibility as a practical question: how do I create accessibility? However, they can also use a further question: what will be the inspirational future for all contained in and symbolised by this technological artefact? Section three is deliberately not a synthesis; this is not a leadership study that seeks to synthesise with other leadership works. Revisiting the quote by Parry and Hansen (2007, p. 282):

> In a criticism of the state of leadership studies, Alvesson and Deetz (2000: 52) wonder if Yukl's (1989) agenda to define 'What is Leadership' could have misled leadership research. They suggest that more might be learned from questions regarding 'what can we see, think, or talk about if we think of leadership as this or that?'

This is the approach of this Element. When we think about the leadership of technology the aim of this work is to give the reader things to 'see', 'think', and 'talk about' – real stories of accessible artefacts that exhibit inspirational leadership for all. The stories are the authentic transformational leadership of technology because they are both innately for the individual and for the general transformational leadership of society. In contrast to perceiving them as disparate technological creations for particular needs, we can now 'think' about accessible technologies as also being for all and containing the common inspirational visions for the future of technology in society. Such gathering of artefacts and celebration of their inspirational leadership has been the central aim of this Element. Thus, we can 'talk about' them as our leadership artefacts no matter who we are; we can see that they symbolise an inspirational future.

Section four is a 'where to now?' section. It takes the lessons learned from charting the course for the transformational leadership of technology through creating accessible artefacts and shows how they could play out.

4. Aiming for the Moon

This section concludes this Element. It offers a future scenario regarding how the leadership of technology through creating accessible artefacts might operate. It is drawn from two incidents at Google. This conclusion makes it clear we can aim for the moon as used in the visual metaphor by Satya Nadella quoted at the beginning of this work.

4.1 The Letter

On 4 April 2018, it was reported by *The New York Times* that in excess of 3,100 Google employees signed a letter to management challenging the company's role in a Pentagon programme (Shane & Wakabayashi, 2018). The details and specifics of the project that the Google employees were protesting has never been made entirely public. What we do know is that the project was titled 'Project Maven'.

The reasons for the passionate and committed pushback by thousands of Google employees is captured in a letter from the employees written to the company's CEO, Sundar Pichai, (cited in Shane & Wakabayashi, 2018). This letter stated that the employees recognised 'Google's moral and ethical responsibility' and that is why the employees demanded that the chief executive 'cancel this project immediately' (cited in Shane & Wakabayashi, 2018).

These Google employees appeared to perceive it their responsibility to challenge the ethics of this contract. In composing the letter and demanding the withdrawal, it appears that they had understood it to be their own moral and ethical responsibility to challenge the use of technology in this context. What is clear from this letter is that these employees had an explicit and well-developed sense of ethical identity.

4.1.1 The Letter's Lesson: The Most Important Question regarding Technology and Leadership for Google Employees

The letter was from some Google employees and it concerned ethics and their identity; however, it was much more than a virtuous statement, although it was this as well. When we look to the instinctual and passionate aspects of the letter, we can imbue that something very significant is at play. These Google employees appear to have realised that AI and technology are products of human talent; moreover, they are a product of this talent's creativity and brilliance. One of the reasons we can imagine or surmise that these employees so forthrightly challenged the Google decision to enter into the Pentagon contract was because they recognised, and indeed could implicitly envisage, the creative and brilliant alternative projects that *could* be undertaken in the future. We can surmise that this strong reaction against the Google contract with the Pentagon occurred not only because these employees questioned the project but also because directing Google talent to the creation of such technology would siphon off brilliant talent, which could be used for other creative projects.

An implicit question raised by thinking about the Google employees' letter provides one of the core leadership challenges for the twenty-first century. That is, how do leaders create workplace structures, spaces, projects, and problems that are worthy of their best creative talent both now and into the future? How do leaders respond to the heartfelt desire, implicit in the Google employees' letter, to have structures that enable the most talented and brilliant to solve meaningful, ethical questions about technology in a practical and creative way? The challenge for leaders is to grapple with these hard questions. This has been part of the aim of this leadership publication. To take the suggestion made by Satya Nadella provided at the beginning of this Element, there needs to be an inspiring vision, a moon to aim for; this metaphorical moon is accessibility and inclusion through technology. This is what, in a sense, the Google employees were desiring in rejecting Project Maven. However, I want to flesh out how this leadership might sound in the real world. To do so, I am going to extrapolate, from a Google Talk, a hypothetical example that creates an accessible technological artefact containing within it an inspiring leadership for all.

4.1.2 The Leadership Hypothetical: 'Is There More That We Could Do?'

Google presents a series that is publicly available on the internet titled Talks at Google. In January of 2017, Google invited Omar Saif Ghobash, who had authored a book titled *Letters to a Young Muslim* (Ghobash, 2017a), to present a talk. Ghobash was ambassador of the United Arab Emirates to Russia when he presented this talk; however, at the time of publication of this text he is ambassador to France. Ghobash acquired his education in Oxford and London in both law and mathematics (Ghobash, 2017b).

Letters to a Young Muslim consists of letters written from a father to his sons. Ghobash was invited to take part in Talks at Google. The description of the book and talk is as follows: 'Today's young Muslims will be tomorrow's leaders and yet too many are vulnerable to extremist propaganda that seems omnipresent in our technological age. The burning question, Ghobash argues, is how moderate Muslims can unite to find a voice ...' (Ghobash, 2017b).

The talk was wide ranging. The aspect of the talk that I want to draw on here is that the ambassador described the importance of literacy in the context of the Middle East, (Ghobash, 2017b, min 12:10) However, he then raised an issue: there is still the problem of what one is to read (Ghobash, 2017b, min 13:29). The broad discussion of the talk, which involved questions and answers, reflected on language, specifically, on how our thinking is often limited or expanded by the concepts that we read and, consequently, how it is important to have access to wide-ranging, humanistic, constructive works of literature and ideas. Ghobash elaborated by speaking about the importance, therefore, of translation in the UAE (Ghobash, 2017b, min 13:35). It was during the question-and-answer period that one of the individuals present at the Google Talk asked the following: '... Is there more that we could do ...?' (Ghobash, 2017b, min 31:25).

If we think back now to the Google employees' letter to the chief executive, which pushed back on the Pentagon contract, we can see an implicit connection to the question above. Google employees, it was surmised in their rejection, were expressing a counter desire to use their talents to ask the question: is there more that we can do? That question speaks of a deep creativity, a sense of wishing to connect the dots of social phenomenon and technology in ways yet unexplored.

When the individual asked, 'Is there more that we could do?' (Ghobash, 2017b, min 31:25), he was presumably aware of the enormity of that question and that there would be no easy answer. This simple question raises interesting practical, social, and multi-disciplinary problems. Therefore, leadership in the twenty-first century essentially is about creating such spaces to ask the question of real problems – Is there more that I can do? – and to deliver practical technological solutions to these creative social questions.

Envisage an imagined Google project focused on literacy and accessibility. The name of this project comes from thinking about the current president of the multilateral Asian Infrastructure Investment Bank, Mr Jin Liqun, who, when he was a young man translated part of Australian Nobel Prize Winner Patrick White's *Tree of Man*. The first line of this book refers to "stringybark", a type of eucalypt tree common in Australia. I often wondered what Mr Jin Liqun, who now has an international leadership role, thought of when he was a young man and read this word. Did he want to travel from China to the Australian landscape and touch a stringybark? Had he seen one before? Do they have stringybark in China? The idea of the "stringybark" became a metaphor for wanting to know and understand something that we don't yet know, to have an engaged, peaceful curiosity. This "Project Stringybark" inspired by the imaginative experience of Mr Jin Liquan and the ideas of translation from Ghobash could create experiences of literary texts, both Middle Eastern and English works, such as stories, great literature, and poetry, by employing and developing Google's machine learning imagery, and sound. In a sense, Google employees could create a whole wealth of intercultural, multisensory, humanistic communication through technology – creating Project Stringybark. Its aim would be to create accessibility and thereby to move beyond simply a translation. Rather to have yet to be imagined, inclusive, diverse expressions and impressions of humanistic stories and increased literacy. This is the essence of the type of project inherent in the question asked at the Google Talk, 'Is there more that we could do?' It would centre on accessibility of literature and literacy. Moreover, the artefact 'Project Stringybark' would contain inspirational leadership. It contains within it a future in which we want to know with an engaged, peaceful curiosity more of each other through our stories. (see the literature referred to in section 1.1).

The above discussion illustrates two challenges in the form of projects, each equally technologically difficult. One is Project Maven, concerning AI and the Pentagon, to be used presumably in landscapes far from Silicon Valley. Project Maven is an artefact and its leadership is in the tradition of defence and security. The other is the imagined Project Stringybark concerning AI stories, literacy, visual and audio (and yet to be imagined expressions of the word). It is an accessible artefact of literature between cultures and its leadership offers an inspiring future to shape the landscapes of our minds with stories.

Both technology projects are technically challenging and possible. The leadership and technology approach dealt with in this Element is one in which the leader creates a place in which talent can flourish so that it can ask questions of society and technology such as, 'Is there more that we could do?' This Element has indirectly answered this question through celebrating the transformational leadership contained in the inspirational motivation of accessible artefacts, thereby giving stories of leadership by which to chart an ethical future for technology.

Visual Conclusion

In Figure 4, a woman is looking at us but, at the same time, she is keen to get back to maths and charting celestial bodies with astronomical instruments. Why does she look at us?

The woman's portrait is housed in the Rijksmuseum, which provides open access and from which the illustration for this Element was drawn. But how did I find her? The description of the image is *Portrait of an Elderly Woman, Seated with Astronomical Instruments*. I would never have found her except I was desperately searching for 'blocks'. It was after looking at what seemed hundreds of images that I saw her: a random gift. She was perfect, literally embodying the idea of charting a celestial body, the moon, which was the metaphor from the Satya Nadella story – the common inspirational destination where accessible artefacts could take us.

Figure 4. Portrait of an elderly woman, seated with astronomical instruments, Amsterdam, c. 1675 – c. 1680

Jan Thopas (Source: Rijksmuseum, Amsterdam)

Further, she embodied the image of leadership; she is quietly charting her science and her destiny. But why search so desperately for blocks? Because I was looking to express the diversity of thought and literacy as expressed by the audio blocks referred to in the Sonocent case study.

And why so desperate for an image?

Because I am dyslexic.

The words you read are shadows of thoughts. They were most directly always first a visual image, a picture, then orally spoken, then typed and then read back. Then, the whole process was repeated over again, and again, and again. Then finally it was sent off for an edit. In these technological, accessible artefacts studied in this Element, I can imagine the personal differences they may make. I need technology.

Technology can assist in the birth of human expressions, inclusion, and dignity. It can also, of course, kill and dominate and create untold effects on society. It is because I have experienced its opening of the space inside that I was dedicated to showing to the general leader the inspirational and transformational leadership contained in accessible technological artefacts, for all. This Element (while a true labour in the medium of the written word) was nevertheless a joyous celebration honouring the silent transformational leadership residing in the artefacts of accessible technologies. I consider myself a celebrator of the symbolic stories created by accessible artefacts.

One last point: when I was to include the wonderful image of charting the future, I thought: who would have drawn a woman in the field of science at that point in history? Given the image was from 1675, I was slightly surprised to have such a powerful woman of science recorded and celebrated.

The artist's name is Jan Thopas. According to Casey and Davies (2017, p. 211), 'his work has only recently come to critical acclaim'. Jan was an artist who was deaf and, in writing about his work, as I googled for information, I found the role of his deafness was celebrated as significant for the power of his work. The authors describe him as having a 'capacity to capture the sensory experience beyond the visual' and 'an uncommon sensory experience of the world'; moreover, he gives a 'sense of silence' (Casey & Davies, 2017, p. 211).

The woman charting commands our attention: she is powerful and has a sense of wanting to be back at work. She smiles (Mona Lisa–like) but with science to get back to. We do not have to imagine her internal life: it is there on display, in her writings in her books, laid on the table before her. She is charting her way forward into these celestial bodies. It is with thanks to the inspiring leadership of the Rijksmuseum that we have access to this woman who sits before us charting and the art work and story of Jan Thopas. I include the image, which is so fitting to the aims of this Element.

References

Accessible Books Consortium. (n.d.a). Accessible Books Consortium Home Page. www.accessiblebooksconsortium.org/portal/en/index.html

Accessible Books Consortium. (n.d.b). Accessible Publishing. www.accessiblebooksconsortium.org/publishing/en/index.html

Accessible Books Consortium. (n.d.c). Capacity Building. www.accessiblebooksconsortium.org/capacity_building/en

Accessible Books Consortium. (2018, 24 September). Accessible Books Consortium: Assemblies 2018 Praised by WIPO DG. https://www.accessiblebooksconsortium.org/news/en/2018/news_0004.html

Alvesson, M., & Deetz, S. (1996). Critical theory and postmodernism approaches to organization studies. In S. R. Clegg, C. Hardy & W. Nord, eds., *Handbook of Organization Studies*, London, United Kingdom: SAGE, pp. 191–217.

Anisman-Razin, M. & Kark, R. (2012). The apple does not fall far from the tree: Steve Jobs's leadership as simultaneously distant and close. In M. C. Bligh & R. Riggio, eds., *When Near is Far and Far is Near: Exploring Distance in Leader–Follower Relationships*. New York, NY: Routledge, pp. 241–73.

Antonakis, J. (2017). "On doing better science: From thrill of discovery to policy implications." *The Leadership Quarterly* 28(1): 5–21.

Antonakis, J. (2018). Charisma and the 'new leadership'. In J. Antonakis & D. V. Day, eds., *The Nature of Leadership*, 3rd ed. Los Angeles, CA: SAGE, pp. 56–81.

Antonakis, J., Bastardoz, N., Jacquart, P. & Sharmir, B. (2016). "Charisma: An ill-defined and ill-measured gift." *Annual Review of Organizational Psychology and Organizational Behavior* 3(1): 293–319.

Bass, B. M. (1985). *Leadership and Performance beyond Expectations*, New York, NY: Free Press.

Bass, B. M. & Bass, R. (2008). *The Bass Handbook of Leadership: Theory Research and Managerial Implications*, 4th ed. Glencoe, IL: Free Press.

Bass, B. M. & Riggio, R. E. (2006). *Transformational Leadership*, 2nd ed. New York, NY: Psychology Press.

Bass, B. M. & Steidlmeier, P. (1999). "Ethics, character, and authentic transformational leadership behaviour." *The Leadership Quarterly* 10(2): 181–217.)

Bligh, M. C. & Riggio, R. (eds.) (2012). *When Near is Far and Far is Near: Exploring Distance in Leader–Follower Relationships*, New York, NY: Routledge.

Boal, K. B. & Schultz, P. L. (2007). "Storytelling, time, and evolution: The role of strategic leadership in complex adaptive systems." *The Leadership Quarterly* 18: 411–28.

Boswell, S. (2010). The Expanding World of Sigrid Cerf. https://leader.pubs.asha.org/doi/10.1044/leader.FTR5.15082010.4

Burns, J. M. (1978). *Leadership*. New York, NY: Harper & Row.

Cancer, M. A., Manzoli, S. & Antonietti, A. (2016). "The alleged link between creativity and dyslexia: Identifying the specific process in which dyslexic students excel." *Cogent Psychology* 3 (1). https://www.cogentoa.com/article/10.1080/23311908.2016.1190309

Cappetta, R. & Gioia, D. (2006). Fine fashion: Using symbolic artifacts, sensemaking and sensegiving to construct identity and image. In A. Rafaeli and M. G. Pratt, eds., *Artifacts and Organizations: Beyond Mere Symbolism*. Mahwah, NJ: Lawrence Erlbaum, pp. 129–219.

Casey, S. & Davies, G. (2017). Drawn away from vision: Encounters with the unseen. In I. Heywood, ed., *Sensory Arts and Design*. London, United Kingdom: Bloomsbury Academic.

Chamayou, G. (2013). A Theory of the Drone, trans. J. Lloyd, New York, NY: The New Press.

Chamberlain, P. J. & Bowen, S. J. (2006). Designers' use of the artefact in human-centred design. In J. Clarkson, P. Langdon and P. Robinson, eds., *Designing Accessible Technology*. London, United Kingdom: Springer, pp. 65–74.

Clarkson, J., Langdon, P. & Robinson, P. (eds) (2006). *Designing Accessible Technology*. London, United Kingdom: Springer.

Cohen, I. (2016). "New Israeli tech sees machines leading the blind". *Jerusalem Post,* 26 September. www.jpost.com/Business-and-Innovation/Tech/Machines-leading-the-blind-468689

Collins, K. (2015). Vodafone instant classroom is digital school in a box for refugees. *Wired.* www.wired.co.uk/article/vodafone-instant-classroom

Cottier, T. (2007). "Preparing for structural reform in the WTO." *Journal of International Economic Law* 10: 497–508.

Cottier, T. (2010). A two-tier approach to WTO decision-making. In D. P. Steger, ed., *Redesigning the World Trade Organization for the Twenty-First Century*. Ottawa, Canada: Wilfrid Laurier University Press, pp. 43–67.

Dijkshoorn, C., ter Weele, W., Jongma, L. & Aroyo, L. (2014). "The Rijksmuseum collection as linked data." *Semantic Web Journal* 1: 7.

Dillet, R. (2017). The OrCam MyEye helps visually impaired people read and identify things. *TechCrunch.* https://techcrunch.com/2017/07/12/the-orcam-myeye-helps-visually-impaired-people-read-and-identify-things/

Eagly, A. H. (2016). "When passionate advocates meet research on diversity: Does the honest broker stand a chance?" *Journal of Social Issues* 72(1): 199–222.

Ellis, G. (2016). Impairment and disability: Challenging concepts of 'normality'. In A. Matamala & P. Orero, eds., *Researching Audio Description: New Approaches*, London, United Kingdom: Palgrave Macmillan, pp. 35–45, doi 10.1057/978-1-137-56917-2_3.

Flanagan, M., Howe, D. & Nissenbaum, H. (2008). Embodying values in technology: Theory and practice. In J. Van den Hoven and J. Weckert, eds., *Information Technology and Moral Philosophy*. Cambridge, United Kingdom: Cambridge University Press, pp. 322–53. doi:10.1017/CBO9780511498725.017.

Gagliardi, P. (1992). *Symbols and artefacts: Views of the corporate landscape*. New York, NY: Aldine de Gruyter.

Garbutt, L. (2019). "How Tennessee Tech improved academic outcomes for students 'at risk of failure'". *Sonocent Blog,* 1 March. https://blog.sonocent.com/2019/03/01/how-tennessee-tech-improved-academic-outcomes-for-students-at-risk-of-failure/2019/

Gaver, B. & Martin, H. (2000) *Exploring Information Appliances through Conceptual Design Proposals*. In Proceedings of CHI 2000, ACM Press.

Ghobash, O. S. (2017a). *Letters to a Young Muslim*. New York, NY: Picador.

Ghobash, O. S. (2017b), Letters to a Young Muslim. Talks at Google. www.youtube.com/watch?v=7BuGDOblyxk

Gladwell, M. (n.d.) Holding Readers: Tools for Engagement, Masterclass, vodcast, viewed 12 September 2020, https://www.masterclass.com/classes/malcolm-gladwell-teaches-writing/chapters/holding-readers-tools-for-engagement#transcript

Greco, G. M. (2016). On accessibility as a human right, with an application to media accessibility. In A. Matamala & P. Orero, eds., *Researching Audio Description: New Approaches*. London, United Kingdom: Palgrave Macmillan, pp. 11–3. doi 10.1057/978-1-137-56917-2_3.

Handler, J., Lobel, O., Mertz, E., Rubin, E. & Simon, W. (2005). "A roundtable on new legal realism, microanalysis of institutions and the new governance: Exploring convergences in differences." *Wisconsin Law Review* 479: 483–4.

Hirsch, M. (2008). "The sociology of international economic law: Sociological analysis of the regulation of regional agreements in the world trading system." *European Journal of International Law* 19, pp. 277–99.

Hohmann, J. & Joyce, D. (eds.) (2018). International Law's Objects, Oxford: Oxford University Press.

Hollander, E. P. (2012). American presidential leadership: Leader credit, follower inclusion, and Obama's turn. In M. C. Bligh & R. Riggio, eds., *When Near is Far and Far is Near: Exploring Distance in Leader–Follower Relationships*. New York, NY: Routledge, pp. 274–313.

Hughes, R. (2012). *The Shock of the New Art and the Century of Change*, London, United Kingdom: Thames and Hudson.

Hughes, T. (2004). *Human-Built World: How to Think about Technology and Culture*. Chicago, IL: University of Chicago Press.

Kalpouzos, I. (2018). Armed Drone. In J. Hohmann and D. Joyce, eds., International Law's Objects, Oxford: Oxford University Press, pp. 118–129.

Korsgaard, C. M. (2008). The Constitution of Agency, Oxford: Oxford University Press.

Koskenniemi, M. (2001). The Gentle Civilizer of Nations: The Rise and Fall of International Law 1870–1960, Cambridge: Cambridge University Press.

LaForgia, R. (2015). "Public participation in the environmental undertaking in the Trans Pacific Partnership a listening approach." *Participatory Educational Research,* Special Issue 2015-1, pp. 145–54.

Latour, B. (1992). Where are the missing masses? The sociology of a few mundane artifacts. In W. Bijker and J. Law, eds., *Shaping Technology/Building Society*, Cambridge, MA: MIT Press, pp. 225–58.

MacKenzie, D. & Wajcman, J. (1985). *The Social Shaping of Technology*, Milton Keynes, United Kingdom: Open University Press.

MacKenzie, S. B. (2003). "The dangers of poor construct conceptualization." *Journal of the Academy of Marketing Science* 31: 323–26.

Mumford, M. D., Connelly, S., Brown, R. P. et al. (2008). "A sensemaking approach to ethics training for scientists: Preliminary evidence of training effectiveness." *Ethics & Behavior* 18: 315–39.

Nadella, S., Shaw, G. & Nichols, J. T. (2017). *Hit Refresh: The Quest to Rediscover Microsoft's Soul and Imagine a Better Future for Everyone*. London, United Kingdom: William Collins.

O'Reilly, T. (2017). *WTF? What's the Future and Why It's Up to Us*. London, United Kingdom: Random House.

Parry, K. W. & Hansen, H. (2007). "The organizational story as leadership." *Leadership* 3(3): 281–300. https://doi.org/10.1177%2F1742715007079309

Pekel, J. (2014). Democratising the Rijksmuseum: Why did the Rijksmuseum make available their highest quality material without restrictions, and what are the results? *Europeana Foundation.* https://pro.europeana.eu/files/

Europeana_Professional/Publications/Democratising%20the%20Rijksmuseum .pdf

Pratt, M. G. & Rafaeli, A. (2001). "Symbols as a language of organizational relationships." *Research in Organizational Behavior* 23: 93–132.

Qizilbash, M. (2009). "Identity, community and justice: Locating Amartya Sen's work on identity in politics." *Politics, Philosophy and Economics* 8 (3): pp. 251–66).

Rafaeli, A. & Pratt, M. G. (2006). Introduction: Artifacts and organizations: More than the tip of the cultural iceberg. In A. Rafaeli and M. G. Pratt, eds., *Artifacts and Organizations: Beyond Mere Symbolism*. Mahwah, NJ: Lawrence Erlbaum, pp. 1–8.

Reha, M., Sloan, D. & Horton, S. (2017). "Accessibility research study: Humanising the need for inclusive design." *Journal of Digital and Social Media Marketing* 5(3): 246–54.

Sanderhoff, M. (2017). Open access can never be bad news. *SMK Open*, 6 March. https://medium.com/smk-open/open-access-can-never-be-bad-news-d33336aad382

Schein, C. H. (2004). *Organizational Culture and Leadership*, Vol. 2, San Francisco, CA: Jossey Bass.

Shane, S. & Wakabayashi, D. (2018). "'The business of war': Google employees protest work for the Pentagon." *The New York Times*, 4 April. www.nytimes .com/2018/04/04/technology/google-letter-ceo-pentagon-project.html

Sekiguchiand, K. & Hori, K. (2018). "Organic and dynamic tool for use with knowledge base of AI ethics for promoting engineers' practice of ethical AI design. *AI and Society* (16 October): 1–21.

Solsman, J. E. (2017). Internet inventor: Make tech accessibility better already. *CNET*, www.cnet.com/news/internet-inventor-vint-cerf-accessibility-disabil ity-deaf-hearing

Steinfeld, E. & Maisel, J. (2012). *Universal Design: Creating Inclusive Environments*. Milton, QLD: John Wiley & Sons.

Thiel, C. E., Bagdasarov, Z., Harkrider, L., Johnson, J. F. & Mumford, M. D. (2012). "Leader ethical decision-making in organizations: Strategies for sensemaking." *Journal of Business Ethics* 107: 49–64.

Tucker, D. (2015). *"Modern technology and software is helping to empower students with dyslexia, 3 ways how." The Independent*, 30 December. www .independent.co.uk/student/student-life/Studies/modern-technology-and-soft ware-is-helping-to-empower-students-with-dyslexia-3-ways-how-a6791131. html

Uhl-Bien, M., Marion, R. & McKelvey, B. (2007). "Complexity leadership theory: Shifting leadership from the industrial age to the knowledge era." *The Leadership Quarterly* 18: 298–318.

United Nations Conference on Trade and Development. (2017). The Gender Dimension of E-commerce, meeting, 27 April, Room XXVI, Palais des Nations, Geneva, Switzerland.

United Nations Convention on the Rights of Persons with Disabilities. (2006). www.un.org/development/desa/disabilities/convention-on-the-rights-of-persons-with-disabilities.html

van Knippenberg, D. & Sitkin, S. B. (2013). "A critical assessment of charismatic-transformational leadership research: Back to the drawing board?" *The Academy of Management Annals* 7(1): 1–60.

Vodafone Group. (2016). Vodafone Foundation launches 'Instant Schools for Africa' to bring advanced educational resources to millions of young Africans. https://www.vodafone.com/news-and-media/vodafone-group-releases/news/instantschools-forafrica

Wakabayashi, D. & Shane, S. (2018). "Google will not renew contract that upset employees." *The New York Times*, 18 June. https://www.nytimes.com/2018/06/01/technology/google-pentagon-project-maven.html

Watts, L. I., Ness, A. M., Steele, M. L. & Mumford, M. D. (2018). "Learning from stories of leadership: How reading about personalized and socialized politicians impacts performance on an ethical decision-making simulation."*The Leadership Quarterly* 29: 276–94.

Wilson, E. J. (2004). Leadership in the digital age. In G. R. Goethals, G. Sorenson & J. MacGregor Burns, eds., *The Encyclopedia of Leadership*. Thousand Oaks, CA: Sage Publications.

Winner, L. (1980). "Do artifacts have politics?" *Daedalus*, 109, (1) (Modern Technology: Problem or Opportunity?), 121–36.

Winner, L. (1986). Do artifacts have politics? In L. Winner, ed., *The Whale and the Reactor: A Search for Limits in an Age of High Technology*. Chicago: University of Chicago Press, pp. 19–39.

World Health Organization. (2019). Disability and Rehabilitation: Global Cooperation on Assistive Technology. www.who.int/disabilities/technology/gate/en/

World Intellectual Property Organization. (2016). Marrakesh Treaty to Facilitate Access to Published Works for Persons Who Are Blind, Visually Impaired or Otherwise Print Disabled. www.wipo.int/treaties/en/ip/marrakesh

Yukl, G. (1989). "Managerial leadership: A review of theory and research." *Journal of Management* 15(2): 251–89.

Cambridge Elements ≡

Leadership

Ronald E. Riggio
Claremont McKenna College

Ronald E. Riggio, Ph.D. is the Henry R. Kravis Professor of Leadership and Organizational Psychology and former Director of the Kravis Leadership Institute at Claremont McKenna College. Dr. Riggio is a psychologist and leadership scholar with over a dozen authored or edited books and more than 150 articles/book chapters. He has worked as a consultant, and serves on multiple editorial boards.

Georgia Sorenson
Churchill College, University of Cambridge

Georgia Sorenson, Ph.D. is the James MacGregor Burns Leadership Scholar at the Moller Institute and Moller By-Fellow of Churchill College at Cambridge University. Before coming to Cambridge, she founded the James MacGregor Burns Academy of Leadership at the University of Maryland, where she was Distinguished Research Professor. An architect of the leadership studies field, Dr. Sorenson has authored numerous books and refereed journal articles.

in partnership with
Møller Centre, Churchill College
www.mollercentre.com

The Møller Institute (www.mollerinstitute.com), home of the James McGregor Burns Academy of Leadership, brings together business and academia for practical leadership development and executive education. As part of Churchill College in the University of Cambridge, the Institute's purpose is to inspire individuals to be the best they can be, to accelerate the performance of the organisations which they serve, and, through our work, to covenant profits to Churchill College to support the education of future leaders. In everything we do our focus is to create a positive impact for people, society, and the environment.

International Leadership Association
www.ila-net.org

The International Leadership Association (www.ila-net.org) is the organisation for connecting leadership scholars, practitioners, and educators in ways that serve to enhance their learning, their understanding, and their impact in the world. These exchanges are professionally enriching, serve to elevate the field of leadership, and advance our mission to advance leadership knowledge and practice for a better world.

About the Series
Elements in Leadership is multi- and inter-disciplinary, and has broad appeal for leadership courses in Schools of Business, Education, Engineering, Public Policy, and in the Social Sciences and Humanities. In addition to the scholarly audience, Elements will appeal to professionals involved in leadership development and training. The series is published in partnership with the International Leadership Association (ILA) and the Møller Institute, Churchill College in the University of Cambridge.

Cambridge Elements ☰

Leadership

Elements in the Series

Printed in the United States
By Bookmasters